THE STORY OF
MANCHESTER

THE STORY OF
MANCHESTER
DEBORAH WOODMAN

In memory of my late grandmothers,
Nancy Kerfoot and Elizabeth Sharp,
whose lives as women were so
very different from my own.

First published 2017

Phillimore, an imprint of The History Press
The Mill, Brimscombe Port
Stroud, Gloucestershire, GL5 2QG
www.thehistorypress.co.uk

British Library Cataloguing in Publication Data.
A catalogue record for this book is available from the British Library.

ISBN 978 0 7509 6780 8

Typesetting and origination by The History Press
Printed and bound in Great Britain by TJ International Ltd

CONTENTS

ABOUT THE AUTHOR

Deborah Woodman has been researching the history of the Manchester region for several years. She has worked at a number of universities in the area, including the University of Salford, University of Manchester, Manchester Metropolitan University and the University of Huddersfield. In 2011, she completed a PhD looking at the role of public houses in nineteenth-century Manchester and Salford, and her specific research interests include the history of drink and leisure, the brewing industry, eighteenth- and nineteenth-century trade and commerce, and nineteenth-century radical politics.

ACKNOWLEDGEMENTS

I have been influenced over the years of researching the history of Manchester by many people and here I would like to thank Professors John Walton and Dave Russell who got me through the PhD and helped me maintain my enthusiasm! I would also like to express appreciation for my mum, Margaret Sharp, who has been a huge personal support over the years while I have combined the day job with my research. My cats Holly and Simba have also been there throughout, sitting by my computer and dragging me away when necessary! They keep me grounded when work becomes stressful.

I wish to thank the following organisations for permission to reproduce images from their collections: the Manchester Central Library for allowing me to publish images from their vast collections, including reproduction of the Ford Madox Brown *Manchester Murals*; the University of Manchester; and the Imperial War Museum. I am also grateful to Norman Redhead of the Greater Manchester Archaeological Unit.

Thanks also to The History Press for enabling me to undertake this book. Finally, I would like to thank the people of Manchester, past and present, for providing such an amazing story to write!

INTRODUCTION

anchester is famous for the 'Industrial Revolution' with its factories, working-class people and rapid urban development, all based around its production of cotton textiles. Whilst this is correct, it is not the complete story. This book traces the development of Manchester and its people from Roman times, since it is here where the story of Manchester begins, when the Romans under the leadership of General Agricola established a garrison at Castlefield. Whilst this was not on the scale of the great Roman cities, it was geographically strategic, and the Romans laid down some of the infrastructure such as major roads seen in central Manchester today, en-route to places such as Chester, Carlisle and York. It is during the medieval period, when William the Conqueror began dispersing lands amongst his barons, that central Manchester developed around the site of the current cathedral, and it is here that the manor of Manchester was built. It is during this time that we see the emergence of textiles as a basis for the local economy, and it is when Flemish textile workers, who were displaced due to war in continental Europe, came to the region, bringing their skills in spinning and weaving. This becomes a major part of the local economy, and the region noted for textiles production, though this was mainly in the woollen trade initially before cotton production took over the region's industry. Manchester was the commercial centre of a network of towns, including Oldham, Rochdale, Bolton and so on, that were active in textile spinning and weaving, and where merchant began meeting each week to trade.

Manchester has always been a place of strong political viewpoints and this is initially displayed during the Civil War of the 1640s where the area largely supported the Parliamentarians, against the monarch Charles I, and despite Royalist efforts to lay siege to the town they were prevented from doing so. The city became noted for radical politics and a people who were not afraid to argue for democracy and justice. Discontent spilled out in the early nineteenth century, since working people were the wealth creators but had no political voice, and the poverty and living conditions were such that they had no choice but to protest; this ultimately led to the Peterloo Massacre, when 16 August 1819 became one of the most notable dates in Manchester's calendar as the cavalry charged a crowd of civilians meeting to hear the radical 'orator' Henry Hunt address the working-class people of Manchester. The people of Manchester were split into two classes and this division was keenly felt in all aspects of daily life. You were either a somebody or a nobody, middle-class or working class, and this shaped your life chances, whether it was your education (or lack of it), type of work, or even whether you went in a beerhouse, pub or an inn. Manchester was the 'shock city' of its age, and observers from far and wide were in awe of what they saw. One of these was the German businessman, Friedrich Engels, who came to Manchester to run the family business in the 1840s, and he wrote his observations in the classic *Conditions of the Working-Class in England*, exposing factory life. Women were faced with limited opportunities in society and, despite men eventually being granted the right to vote, women had to fight long and hard into the twentieth century before they had equal democratic rights to men. Here, it was mainly educated middle-class women, such as Lydia Becker and Emmeline Pankhurst who fought this battle.

Manchester during the twentieth century was badly affected by war, like many other places. The city recruited volunteers for the First World War and sent one of the largest Pals regiments to the front line. During the Second World War, central Manchester and nearby Trafford Park were devastated in the Christmas Blitz of 1940. By the turn of the First World War the cotton industry was already in decline and struggling to compete with other countries that had invested in newer technology in the industry. The wars turned a struggling industry into a virtually non-existent one, and in the aftermath of post-war reconstruction Manchester had to reinvent its economy to provide employment and prosperity. This took some time and it was not until the 1980s that the city returned to the cosmopolitan centre of opportunity it had once been.

Manchester has also been a place of culture. From the nineteenth century the middle class created a host of literary and scientific institutions, such as the Portico Library, the Manchester Art Gallery and the Literary and Philosophical Society. In 1857, the Art Treasures Exhibition was one of the grandest displays of art and industry ever seen in Britain. Into the twentieth century, Manchester has been the home of a range of musical trends from the Hallé Orchestra to the Hacienda nightclub, where classical music has sat beside punk and new genre pop and rock music. The Hallé still exists, yet the Hacienda provided a brief moment in popular culture, but whose cultural legacy in popular music continues. Manchester is also a sporting city that is home to two of the most famous football clubs in the UK if not the world, and is also home to Lancashire County Cricket. The success of the Commonwealth Games in 2002 also placed Manchester firmly on the sporting map as a place for athletics, where top-class facilities and elite athletes allow competition at the highest level.

The history of Manchester is very much based around its people, who were often pioneers, whether this be the development of the first railway line from Manchester to Liverpool in 1830, the first public library created in the seventeenth century by the legacy of Humphrey Chetham and subsequently the first publicly funded library at Campfield in 1851, fighting for greater political rights, or becoming the key wealth creators for the nation. As we advance through the twenty-first century, Manchester's role in the United Kingdom remains undiminished as it becomes ever more cosmopolitan and a northern powerhouse of economic, social and political progress. Here is its story.

Deborah Woodman, 2017

one

MANCUNIUM

Manchester had a Roman foundation, though not worth lingering on about. Its only standing structural remains, the fragment of a wall in a goods yard at the bottom of Deansgate, must rank as the least interesting Roman remain in England, which is setting a high standard.

A.J.P. Taylor (1957)

Introduction

Whilst Manchester cannot make high claims of vast quantities of well-preserved Roman architecture such as that seen in York and Chester, it was of strategic Roman importance as the home of a military garrison and it certainly marks the beginning of the story of Manchester, since it was here that the foundations of one of Britain's greatest cities were laid. This chapter looks at a range of archaeological evidence from a number of excavations over the centuries to establish why Manchester became a strategic military site, where the Romans settled, and how the Roman period laid the foundations for a city that was centuries away from the major industrial and cultural centre that we know today. Finally, the chapter will uncover why the site was so important to the Romans in their quest for domination of the British Isles and the legacy they left behind.

The Origins of Mancunium

Manchester's name has had a number of variations over the years, including Mancunium and Mamucium, and whose origins can be traced from around AD 48 to 79 until around the fourth century AD, though Mancunium is the more recognisable name that we associate with Manchester, where locals are still known as Mancunians, and even a key motorway through the centre of Manchester is the Mancunian Way.[1] The legacy of Roman Manchester is still present, mainly through the Romans roads and geography which still form the basic structure of the city, yet we are largely oblivious to this as we wander around Deansgate, Castlefield, Great Bridgewater Street and Liverpool Road. The Roman military station occupied a strategic position close to the rivers Medlock and Irwell that became known as Castlefield, and it is here that the remains and reconstructions of the site can be found. It was a small but important strategic military site, and in order to establish why Manchester became a Roman garrison town it is necessary to look at the wider geography and people of north-west England. Before the Roman occupation, the region is known to have been inhabited by the Brigantes, a Celtic tribe whose name reflected the terrain they occupied. 'Brigantes' meant free, high or upland people and they occupied an area that stretched from Hadrian's Wall in the north to the more southerly Peak District. The Manchester region was known to have been the home of a particular group of the Brigantes, known as the Setantii. There is little evidence available that sheds light on the relationship that existed between the Brigantes and their Roman conquerors, since most archaeological evidence was left by the Romans and not the people they conquered. However, what has remained has suggested a positive alliance between the Brigantes tribe and the Romans.[2] The Brigantian chief, Queen Cartimandua, appeared not to have been especially hostile to the Romans, and the region the Brigantes tribe inhabited became an area that shielded the territory that the Romans occupied against more hostile northern tribes that were not so accommodating to their conquerors.

The Roman conquest of Britain began around AD 43 under the direction of Emperor Claudius and the occupation lasted for around 400 years. The Romans did not assert control over northern England until the AD 70s, since by around AD 47 they had become somewhat stuck along the Fosse Way, a Roman road that linked Exeter with Lincoln, and it was not until around AD 77 when their Roman leader, Gnaeus Julius Agricola, arrived in Britain that

1 Statue of Agricola above the door of Manchester Town Hall.

they made further progress. Agricola eventually led the Roman armies to the north, where after a brief campaign in North Wales he turned his attention to north-west England, bringing his Twentieth Legion to Chester and eventually making progress towards York. Agricola was known to personally choose military sites, and often these were squares of around 3 to 5 acres and capable of holding around 500 soldiers. The site at Castlefield fitted this description well. According to Tacitus, the Roman writer and brother-in-law of Agricola, the army under Agricola's leadership attacked the Brigantes forcefully, but in order to maintain his control over them he developed shrewd political skills by offering concessions to the locals in order to gain their acceptance and cooperation. The garrison's construction was part of a programme to overpower the native tribes, but at the same time it is evident that the Brigantian state had already started to decline. The indigenous population formed settlements around the garrison in an area close to the current Deansgate that became known as Alport, or old town.

The Roman Garrison

Castlefield was chosen for a number of strategic reasons. In addition to being the correct shape and size for Agricola's army, it also had other geographical features that made it a good military position. First, the land on which the garrison was built was located on a high sandstone outcrop that was surrounded by curves in the rivers Medlock and Irwell. The site has been referred to as *Mamucium* or 'breast-like hill' because of its shape, and it is here that this other Roman name for Manchester originated. The garrison was on a junction with Watling Street, the great Roman road that crossed the country, and here one part of it went from Manchester to Cumbria. Other roads that the Romans created emanated directly from the garrison, making it a place of strategic military importance, particularly on the main arterial routes between the two of the major Roman military bases and settlements west to east between Chester and York, thereby servicing major Roman settlements either side of the Pennines, and on the main arterial route north to Carlisle.[3] The road north to another notable Roman town, Ribchester, was routed via Bridgewater Street, Liverpool Road, along Deansgate and towards the north of the region.[4] Roads between Manchester and Chester were known to have existed from around AD 74, close to the Castlefield site, which added a further incentive for the garrison to be situated here.[5] The road to Chester was known to have followed a route via the River Medlock close to Great Jackson Street, through Hulme and Stretford towards Broadheath. The road to the other great Roman city of York took a route via Great Bridgewater Street, towards Ancoats, then following on to Newton Heath and up towards Oldham and over the Pennines where the other Roman site of the area, Castleshaw, can be found. On the north side of the garrison, a number of smaller streets were created around the Camp Street, Quay Street and Lower Byrom Street areas, where it seems likely that there were settlements to support the garrison itself and occupied by soldiers and traders.[6]

The garrison itself was built around AD 79, ironically around the same time that Pompeii and Herculaneum were destroyed by the infamous eruption of Vesuvius in the Bay of Naples, and was known to be occupied for a little over 300 years. Excavations have revealed a number of key changes throughout its existence and it appears to have been rebuilt on three separate occasions before being abandoned around AD 410. The first stage of construction around AD 79 was subsequently redeveloped somewhere in the region of AD 160, with further work around AD 200.[7] During the first century, the garrison appears to have been built mainly of timber and designed to house around 500 soldiers, but by the early second century it was replaced with a stone structure that could house around 1,000 soldiers and developed further to incorporate stone gateways and walls. Specifically, there is evidence that the site was redeveloped between AD 110 and AD 160, when it was enlarged, probably to incorporate a range of granaries since a site of this nature needed suitable stores of food to provide for the soldiers who were making attempts to move further into northern England, and particularly during the winter months, which the Romans were not especially used to. The garrison was surrounded by a ditch and stone rampart and was about 5 acres in size. There are also likely to have been towers at regular intervals along the ramparts, and the inside would have contained regimental headquarters, barracks for the soldiers, stables and other stores for food and supplies, and this can be ascertained both from the limited finds on the site and from what other Roman garrisons looked like.

Archaeological evidence has also been found to indicate the presence of baths and hypocausts to provide underfloor heating. Figure 2 depicts the geography of the site and how it may have looked around AD 200, showing the garrison next to the bend in the river and the settlements that developed around. The whole site that contained the garrison was known as the *Castellum* and the River Irwell ran north–south of the *Castellum*, which provided a further

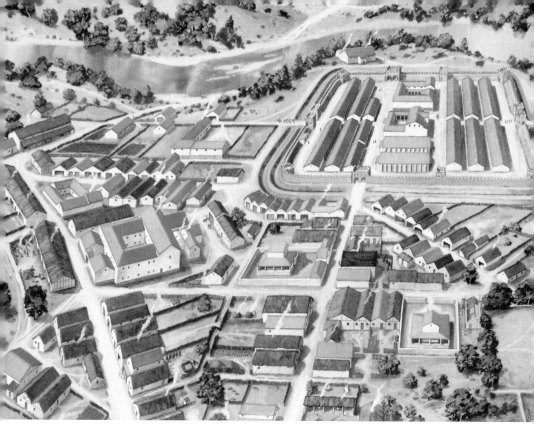

2 Reconstruction of Roman Manchester as it might have appeared around AD 200. (By Graham Sumner based on advice from Norman Redhead, County Archaeologist)

line of defence, where it was also circled by the rivers Tib and Medlock.[8] Some buildings that existed have been replicated to give an indication of what the site may have looked like, and these include a reconstruction of the garrison's North Gate. Figures 3 to 5 show either side of the North Gate as it may have looked, where the reconstruction on the original Roman foundations was built in 1982 following an excavation of the site. By the middle of the second century the rectangular fort contained four gateways, with one on each side.

The North Gate was built on a Roman road that ran into the area that was inhabited by the civilian population. This outer civilian area was known as the *vicus*, and archaeologists have found evidence of life around the garrison that includes iron working workshops that were vital for producing weapons. The garrison utilised natural resources in the area and developed a number of trades to support the soldiers and their families, and included blacksmiths and bakehouses, for example. In some of the excavations, hearths suitable for metal working were discovered and a pottery kiln was found in nearby Tonman Street. Other buildings that have been excavated include three Roman buildings which lay aside the Roman road that ran from the North Gate, and it has been suggested that these could have been a shop, an inn and a house. Most were of timber construction on a stone foundation, with either a thatch or tile roof and clay daub walls. A water mill was constructed close by the River Medlock. Sheep fleeces were turned into clothing, providing a distinct advantage in northern England's mild and damp climate that could turn cold in winter. It is estimated that the *vicus* was home to around 2,000 people around AD 200 and covered the area from Quay Street to Deansgate. Figures 6 and 7 show the foundations of Roman buildings set outside the fort, next to a Roman road.

The back of the North Gate, close to today's Duke Street, contains reconstructions of the western wall and ramparts. This site was thought to have been used to provide aggregates for both building the garrison and later creating ditches that were utilised for defensive purposes. Excavations have revealed that the ditches were filled with discarded pottery dating around the second century AD. The area also contained a granary to store food including grain and meat. This had a raised floor to provide ventilation and keep the grain dry. Normally a garrison would have contained two granaries that could keep the community supplied with food for a year. The rampart was supported by a stone structure and it is thought this survived until the end of the Roman occupation. Figure 8, showing the western walls and ramparts, reveals how close the Roman site was to the Victorian railway building area, where a good deal of archaeology was destroyed in the railway construction of the 1830s and 1840s.

There are a number of eye-witness descriptions of Castlefield that date back to the sixteenth century and these give us some brief insights into the remains that existed some 500 years or so after the Roman occupation, and despite this lapse in time, they add to our understanding of what the site may have looked like. The testimonies that have survived over the centuries include those of John Leland, William Camden, John Horsley and William Stukeley. The earliest observation we have is that of John Leland, who was one of the Henry VIII's antiquaries, whose tours of England led him to the region in the 1530s. The old English in which it is written can be difficult to read, but he states how:

> And almost ii flyte shottes withowt the towne beneth on the same syde of Irwel yet be seene the dikes and fundations of Old Man Castel yn a ground now inclosed. The stones of the ruines of this castel wer translatid towards making of bridgges for that toune.[9]

Above 3 & 4 Reconstruction of the North Gate.

Left 5 The inscription on the North Gate commemorates the detachment of Raetious, the Noricans and Lucius Senecanius Martius.

Above 6 & 7 Reconstructed foundations of buildings in the civilian *vicus* area.

Right 8 Reconstruction of the western walls and ramparts.

This description, whilst suggesting that there were visible ruins, does not elaborate on what was actually there, apart from evident archaeological remains, though he does indicate a self-contained site where some of the rubble left from the site was redeployed into the building of bridges in the centre of Manchester, which no doubt had a negative effect on the remaining archaeology. The second observation is that of the historian William Camden, who visited during the 1620s:

> In a neighbouring park belonging to the Earls of Derby, call'd Alparc, I saw the foundations of an old square Fort, which they call *Mancastle*; where the river Medloc joins the Irwell. I will not say, that this was the ancient Mancunium, the compass of it is so little; but rather it was some Roman station.[10]

Later descriptions include that of the archaeologist and antiquarian John Horsley from around the early eighteenth century and a more comprehensive analysis by Dr William Stukeley, a member of the clergy who also had an interest in archaeology. Both were commenting in the early eighteenth century. First, Horsley stated that:

> When I was at Manchester, I examined with care the Roman station west from it. The field in which it stands is called Castle-field. The river runs near it, on the east side. The ramparts are still very conspicuous.[11]

The description offered by Horsley does suggest that there was some meaningful archaeology remaining but Stukeley goes much further, commenting in 1723:

> A Roman Castrum was on the west side going for Chester by Stretford, and on the northern bank of the river Medlock. It is a small piece of level ground, somewhat higher than that around it. It does not cover the whole piece, but is a square, 500 feet one way, 400 the other; nor can it be said to be ditched about, but the ground beside it for some distance is manifestly removed into the castle, and spread long its verge, not as a regular vallum, but sloping inwards; by this means the area of it is higher on the sides that the middle, and the exterior ground is lowered around to the foot of the castle, which is steep, like the sides of the vallum. Upon this edge there has been a wall, quite round; the foundations of it are to be discovered almost everywhere, in some places large parcels of are left but not above ground. Now they call it Castle Croft.[12]

Another form of representation of the Roman garrison comes from the nineteenth-century artist, Ford Madox Brown, who painted a scene depicting the arrival of the Romans in Manchester as part of his collection of the *Manchester Murals* housed in the Great Hall of Manchester Town Hall. His work is not meant as an accurate recreation of Castlefield but is a symbolic piece of art that represents the start of Manchester's story. The term *Mancenion* referred to in the title of his work is another incarnation of Manchester's original name and here this is believed to have been an ancient Briton term meaning *place of tents*. Madox Brown discusses his thoughts when undertaking the painting:

> This subject embodies the foundation of Manchester; for, although the British name 'Mancenion' seems to indicate this locality as a centre for population, it is improbable that anything worthy the name of a town existed before the Roman Mancunium. Agricola was Governor of Britain at this date AD 60 and was, as his son-in-law Tacitus informs us, a humane as well as an energetic Governor. His rule was much connected with this part of England, so that the general depicted may be considered as representative of that Governor. A centurion holds the parchment plan of the camp that is being fortified, while his chief, who also has hold of it, gives his orders. His standard-bearer, in this instance a 'Dragonifer,' holds up the

9 Ford Madox Brown, *The Romans Building a Fort at Mancenion.* (Courtesy of Manchester Libraries, Information and Archives, Manchester City Council)

silken wind-inflated Dragon standard which the Romans at this period had adopted from the 'Barbarians.' The legionaries are doing the masons' work; but the bearers of stones and cement are Britons, impressed for the occasion. The River Medlock bounds the camp on the south; the background beyond it is formed of oak forests, red with the last leaves of November, while in the extreme distance is visible the blue streak of the distant Peak hills. A chilling wind is depicted as agitating the garments of the conquerors, and making the work in hand more arduous to men of southern nationality.[13]

Excavations and Finds

There have been a number of examinations and excavations at Castlefield, the earliest of which was conducted by John Whitaker in the 1770s, followed by later work carried out by Charles Roeder and Francis Bruton at the end of the nineteenth and turn of the twentieth centuries.[14] More recent work, such as that by Barrie Jones in the 1970s and excavations in the 1980s and 2000s by the Greater Manchester Archaeological Unit, have all added to our over-all understanding of the garrison. Consequently, over the centuries there have been a number of important finds that have enabled us to form a picture of life in the garrison and surrounding area. Even some prehistoric remains have been found in more recent excavations but there are too few finds to allow us to form a coherent picture of life before the Romans arrived. However, they do indicate that there was some form of habitation of the site around Castlefield before the Roman occupation. These finds included an early bronze-age flint found on Barton Street and two mesolithic flints and a further bronze-age flint from the Liverpool Road area. There were also some redeposited pieces of bronze iron-age pottery found in the vicinity.

However, it is clear that urban development of the eighteenth and nineteenth centuries badly affected the site, since many of the remaining structures were destroyed when new buildings, canals and railways were constructed as part of the Industrial Revolution. In particular, the site was damaged by the construc-tion of the Bridgewater Canal in the 1760s, followed by the railways around Liverpool Road station during the 1830s and 1840s. The construction of a railway viaduct near Liverpool Road during this time effectively destroyed the core of the garrison itself, and other subsequent urban development severely damaged evidence that would have offered us a deeper understanding of life in Roman Manchester. Archaeologist Charles Roeder concluded that it was the building of the Altrincham railway in 1849, cutting through the site, that destroyed much of the foundations and archaeology, and he complained that officials of the time did not allow archaeologists to investigate the site before the railway construction began. It is unfortunate that 300 to 400 years of Roman habitation was lost very quickly during the late eighteenth and nineteenth centuries.[15]

Despite this, some artefacts did indeed survive and some were found whilst construction work was taking place. One of the first ever major finds was as far back as 1612 when a Roman altar was discovered under the root of an oak tree growing on the river bank near Knott Mill, and is believed to have been found near the site of the Roman baths. It is thought that this altar was created in honour of the goddess Fortuna by an officer called Senecianius in the Roman army. For most of the time since it was found, the altar has been housed in Oxford's Ashmolean Museum, but more recently has been on loan to the Manchester Museum.[16] In 1808, a number of Roman dishes were found at Castlefield, owing to construction work of the Rochdale Canal, close to the junction with the Bridgewater Canal. They had been well preserved and undisturbed for many hundreds of years, and, not realising the significance of the finds, workmen took them for scrap value and it is only by chance that they were rescued and put with the collections at the British Museum.[17] Later finds include some Roman coins from the years AD 306 to 340 at the Manchester side of Salford Bridge, which was the area around the current Manchester Cathedral, and some have suggested that there may have been a Roman site there too, but not enough evidence has been found to support this theory. A more significant artefact was discovered in 1839 during the construction of the Hall of Science in Tonman Street and proved to be one of the most notable Roman finds ever found in Manchester, that of a bronze statuette of Jupiter Stator and a silver coin of Trajan, which dated from around AD 98 to 117. Equally interesting and important were the discovery of two further bronze statuettes of Hercules and Genius of Mauritania. Other finds included more coins, weapons, lamps, tiles, glass ware and a range of pottery.[18] It is also believed that a cemetery was located south-east of the garrison. Some of the information about this site comes from Whitaker's examination of the area, who maintained that during the 1760s urns containing seemingly human remains were found. In 1832, a wooden coffin was found near the River Medlock, and in 1849 excavations took place around the cemetery area, but sadly none of the remains are with us today.[19]

John Whitaker undertook one of the first detailed examinations of the site during the early 1770s. Whitaker was local to Manchester and spent much of his life as a clergyman and historian. Inspired by a number of Roman finds as a result of the 1760s construction of the Bridgewater Canal, he investigated Castlefield in some depth and subsequently published his findings in a series of volumes of *The History of Manchester* between 1771 and 1775, alongside a range of works on the Roman Empire. In his history of the area he stated:

> The parish of Manchester was originally a wild, unfrequented tract of woodland, inhabited merely by the bear, the bull, and the wolf, and traversed only by the hunters of the neighbouring country. In the first visit of the Romans to Britain, under Julius Caesar it does not appear that the invaders penetrated so far north as Lancashire and it was not till the time of Agricola (AD 79) that Manchester passed under Roman yoke. At that period the tumults of war were introduced amongst the peaceable inhabitants, and Manchester was occupied by the levies from the banks of the Tiber. A Roman station was constructed in the Castlefield near the confluence of the Medlock with the Irwell; and another (and smaller) establishment about a mile to the north of it at the confluence of the Irk with the same river, received a colony of inhabitants who made it their summer residence. Four minor fortresses were placed for their protection within and the woodland were intersected with Roman roads, all ranging at right angles through the thickets and converging to a point in the Castlefield.[20]

Whitaker was both commended and criticised in equal measure. Some considered his work to be a welcome look at Manchester's early history, but others have criticised his over-generalisations and claims with no supporting evidence. However, his descriptions of the remains of the walls at the site were seen to be accurate. The most important (and some would say more academic) archaeological excavations began at Castlefield with the work carried out by Charles Roeder from 1897 to 1900. A detailed examination of his findings is offered in his work *Roman Manchester* which he produced in 1900. Roeder was an amateur archaeologist but his work was detailed and systematic and he uncovered a good number of pottery fragments, and claims to have found around 500 pieces of the highly prized red Samian pottery that the Romans used, which was a high-quality porcelain type of pottery that was usually red in colour and decorated in the finest details, ownership of which demonstrated status and affluence. The presence of this kind of pottery, such as jars and urns, and the

quality of the finds are indicators that the inhabitants had a comfortable existence.[21] Francis Bruton undertook a further excavation of the garrison in 1907.
This work was important because the site was again facing further damage since
the land was scheduled for redevelopment and additional railway construction,
so the archaeological team had to quickly complete their work. This excavation
was important in revealing more details of the Roman garrison. Collectively,
the archaeology uncovered by both Roeder and Bruton included ramparts of
the garrison and revealed a more important and extensive walled area. Bruton's
team discovered further coins, tiles and a Samian vase. They also found a granary that was located inside the *Castrum*, allowing for the storage of provisions,
particularly important for times such as winter or a military siege, and reinforced the fort's military importance.[22] In terms of other key finds, a *mortarium*,
a Roman kitchen bowl which had a rough surface so that substances could be
ground to a fine powder, was found, alongside red Samian pottery 'with foliage
and birds, and with a wonderful glaze on it'.[23] The floor was found to be of red
sandstone. Around 100 coins were found and thirty-eight were identified as
being in the time of Emperors Claudius and Nero through to Antoninus Pius,
and this leads experts to the conclusion that Roman occupation may have in
fact began a little earlier than previously thought at around AD 60, a date that
links Manchester more with activity around Chester than York. Also, the last
emperor seen on the coins, Pius, led archaeologists to consider that the garrison was occupied until around the end of the second century AD, though
another theory is that the site was still in existence but no longer used for military occupation.[24] The area around Knott Mill contained a large building, and
a Roman well is believed to have been located near the more recent Crown Inn
public house on Trafford Street. Remarkably, and despite much destruction of
the archaeology, some Roman glass survived and was found in a location just
off Cateaton Street close to the cathedral.[25] The excavations by Roeder, Bruton
and others have challenged John Whitaker's more flamboyant assertions, the
most notable being a disagreement over the significance of artefacts discovered
in the area around the cathedral. Roeder was especially critical of Whitaker's
analysis, and disputed his claims that the Romans held a summer camp at this
location. The debate has continued about whether the Romans occupied the
site that formed medieval Manchester, and despite some finds it has not been
proven either way.

More modern archaeological surveys include that conducted by Professor
Barrie Jones of the University of Manchester's Archaeological Unit in the

10 The Chester Road Roman altar found in 2008. (Norman Redhead, Greater Manchester Archaeological Advisory Service)

1970s. Their first examination was in 1972, when the team examined the *vicus*, the focus of this excavation being either side of White Lion Street, an area that currently forms the Roman Gardens just off Liverpool Road. A further excavation in 1977 was undertaken in nearby Byrom Street and Tonman Street.[26] This revealed sections of a Roman road that linked the North Gate with the road to Ribchester, and further evidence was uncovered of everyday life at the garrison, including workshops, hearths and furnaces. The Greater Manchester Archaeological Unit's work during the 1980s and early 2000s has also added to our understanding with new finds, which include a metre-high Roman altar, found in 2008 at the junction between Chester Road and Great Jackson Street, which depicts Aelius Victor, a Roman soldier, who made the altar as an offering to two minor Roman goddesses. The Latin inscription says: 'To the mother goddesses Hananeftis and Ollototis, Aelius Victor willingly and deservedly fulfils a vow'. It had been concluded that Victor could have been an army officer in the second half of the second century AD and the altar may have represented thanks for something good that may have happened to him. It is known to be made from Pennine millstone grit, and on top there is a small bowl shape where oil or other liquids could be placed by way of an offering. The altar was found in an ancient rubbish pit on the site of a former garage, together with a Samian bowl decorated with a hunting scene and dating from around AD 150. In all, it is estimated that the excavations of the garrison and surrounding area have uncovered around 10,000 artefacts.[27]

The End of the Fort

So, what happens to the garrison and why did it end? It appears to have been abandoned between 200 to 300 years after its occupation.[28] More precisely, evidence from the site suggests that the site was largely abandoned by the middle of the third century AD.[29] The civilian *vicus* around the garrison appears to have been unoccupied from around the middle of the third century, and fits with the date following the end of Roman rule in the north-west of England, which occurred around AD 383, and the eventual collapse of the Roman Empire itself. By the AD 420s, Britain's Roman conquerors had all but disappeared. It appears that Roman soldiers were required elsewhere in a bid to keep the faltering empire going, but it was destined to fail as the empire had totally outreached its capabilities and the limits to which the frontiers of the empire could be managed, so far away from its headquarters in Rome. There was no sudden end to the Roman occupation of Britain, but rather it was a slow demise of an empire that was crumbling at its heart in Italy and finding it increasingly hard to manage its provinces. In fact, Italy itself was the subject of attack, and many troops in the outlying areas were called back to their homeland to defend their country. The Romans in Britain also became too stretched, as their numbers were increasingly limited to keeping out the Anglo-Saxons and Picts that made repeated raids on the British mainland, and it is these tribes that form the next part of Manchester's history.

Conclusion

The chapter began with an unflattering quote by the notable historian A.J.P. Taylor that certainly does not do justice to the beginning of Manchester's story and the arrival of the Romans during the first decades AD. Whilst the site was small compared to other Roman towns in Britain, it was of strategic importance and laid down a basic infrastructure of roads that formed the basis of Manchester's main thoroughfares that we follow to the present day. It is unfortunate that there is not more evidence that we can call upon to investigate Mancunium in more detail, as industrial progress negatively impacted on the preservation of the area's heritage. The departure of the Roman army, following the subsequent fall of the Roman Empire, left a gap in the historical record as to what happened to the site next, as the next pieces of evidence we have are the descriptions by Leland, Camden and Stukeley. Despite the destruction caused by nineteenth-century construction of canals, railways and buildings there have been a number of excavations to piece together life in Roman Manchester, and these have yielded some fascinating insights into the garrison and civilian life around it. Today, what remains of the site has been preserved, and reconstructed in places, to give an indication of just how important this site was in the beginning of Manchester's story. As the Romans left the area 300 or so years after their arrival around AD 79, there is a gap in Manchester's history and much of the conjecture that is written on the post-Roman period is the focus of the next chapter.

Notes

1 Bryant, S., Morris, M., Walker, J.S.F., *Roman Manchester: a frontier settlement* (Greater Manchester Archaeological Unit, 1986), ch. 2.
2 Bryant, Morris, Walker, *Roman Manchester*, ch. 2.
3 Jones, B., Grealey, S., *Roman Manchester* (Sherratt for the Manchester Excavation Committee, 1974), ch.1.
4 Axon, W., *The Annals of Manchester* (John Heywood, 1885). pp. 1–2.
5 Axon, *The Annals of Manchester*, pp. 1-2.
6 Roeder, C., *Roman Manchester* (Richard Gill, 1900), p. 50.
7 Connelly, P., *73/83 Liverpool Road, Manchester: An archaeological excavation within the roman vicus – excavation report* (University of Manchester Archaeological Unit, 2002).
8 Roeder, *Roman Manchester*, p. 50.
9 Toulmin-Smith, L., *The Itinerary of John Leland in or about the years 1535–1543* (George Bell & Sons, 1909), p. 6.

10 Camden, W., *Britannia*, (translated from Latin by Edmund Gibson), (University of Adelaide e-books, 1722).

11 Baines, T., *Lancashire and Cheshire: past and present*, vol. 1 (Heritage Publications (1868 (2012)), p. 266.

12 Baines, E., *History of the County Palatine of Lancaster* (George Routledge & Sons, 1868), p. 152.

13 Hueffer, F., *Ford Madox Brown: a record of his life and work* (Longmans, 1896), pp. 338–9.

14 Bruton, F.A., *The Roman Fort at Manchester* (Manchester University Press, 1909); Roeder, *Roman Manchester;* Whitaker. J., *The History of Manchester,* vol. 1 (Dodsley, White & Lowndes, 1771).

15 Roeder, *Roman Manchester,* p. 55.

16 Swindells, T., *Manchester Streets and Manchester Men* (vol. 1) (J E Cornish, 1906), pp. 140–2.; In 2016 the altar could be found in Manchester Museum.

17 Baines, *History of the County*, p. 269.

18 Swindells, *Manchester Streets*, vol 1, pp. 140–2.

19 Jones and Grealey, *Roman Manchester*, p. 17.

20 Baines, *History of Lancashire*, p. 267.

21 Roeder, *Roman Manchester*, p. 51.

22 *Manchester Courier* 7 January 1907.

23 *Manchester Courier* 8 January 1907.

24 *Manchester Courier* 31 January 1907.

25 Roeder, *Roman Manchester*, p. 95.

26 Gregory, R., *Roman Manchester: the University of Manchester's Excavations within the Vicus, 2001–5* (Oxbow Books, 2007), p. 3.

27 Gregory, *Roman Manchester*, p. 181.

28 *Manchester Courier*, 6 November 1866.

29 Gregory, *Roman Manchester*, p. 54.

two

FROM MEDIEVAL VILLAGE TO EARLY MODERN TOWN

The history of Manchester is of some succeeding years little more than a blank, and it therefore be conjectured that the town was progressing favourably, since it is generally found that those times which present fewest incidents worthy of commemoration, are the richest in actual comfort and prosperity to the people.

James Wheeler (1836)

Introduction

This chapter looks at Manchester's development from medieval village to early modern town, from the quiet that transpired after the Roman occupation had ended to when Manchester emerges as a manorial town, whose governance was through barons that had acquired status and land, seeking favour from the monarchs of the day. It is during this period that the origins of what was to become the modern city become visible, with the development of trade and commerce that would ultimately make the city famous in later centuries. This chapter takes the story from around AD 500 through to around the 1550s. However, most of the information we have is from the eleventh century, from which the historian can draw upon more in the way of historical records, particularly from the period after the Norman Conquest of 1066, and it is from this date that the development of the manor of Manchester can be traced, when William the Conqueror's reign was felt throughout the land, and with the rise of key families that begin to dominate and rule Manchester. The Collegiate Church, which was an important feature of local life, develops next to the manor and today this is known as Manchester Cathedral. It was during this time that textiles became an important aspect of the local economy as Flemish weavers come to the region to avoid persecution due to European continental wars, bringing their skills in textile production. The issue of trying to piece together aspects of local medieval life, owing to limited archival evidence, and building up a picture of life during this time is filled with conjecture and local tales that have been handed down. However, what evidence there is does provide us with vital insights into how Manchester developed, and here is the story of Mamecester, as the town became known in medieval times.

The Romans Depart

After the Romans departed the area, the historical record as to what happened next and who took their place becomes patchy and flimsy, and much of the evidence available is often filled with uncertainty. A local legend that has been handed down is the story of Tarquin's Castle and tales of conflict between local knight Tarquin and Sir Lancelot in the legends of King Arthur. This tale was originally recited by local historian Richard Hollingworth in his 1656 work *Mancuniensis*, which is one of the earliest histories of Manchester, but there is no evidence that this story has any truth in it. However, it is a lively tale worth reciting:

> It is said that Sir Tarquine, a stout enemie of King Arthur, kept his castle, and neere to the foard in medlock, about mab-house hung a bason on a tree on which bason whoever did strike, Sir Tarquine, or some of his company, would come and fight with him, and that sir Launcelot du lake, a Knight of King Arthur's round table, did beate upon the bason, fought with Tarquine, killed him, possessed himself of the castle and loosened the prisoners.[1]

Hollingworth goes on to discuss the legend and the story of King Arthur. The nineteenth-century historian William Axon also makes reference to this story in his 1885 work *The Annals of Manchester,* and he describes the events as taking place around AD 520, also referring to a local legend that Tarquin, an enemy of King Arthur, kept a castle at Manchester, but was killed by Lancelot.[2] He also casts serious doubt on the story as a whole, but it is a romantic tale that has stood the test of time to become part of local folklore, and has been published as *The Ancient Ballad of Tarquin.*[3]

The gap in government and leadership left by the Romans was filled by a number of invading tribes from both Scotland and mainland Europe that settled in the British Isles, and these included the Picts, since the somewhat dispersed indigenous Britons were insufficient in number and organisation to halt the advancing Picts and Scots. Another group of invaders were the Saxons, a Germanic tribe that arrived in Britain from the mid-fifth century and success-fully cleared out the other invaders, and one theory behind their arrival suggests that the Britons invited the Saxons to England to protect them from these northern invading tribes. Under Saxon rule, the church and the market were a key part of their communities and villages, turning them into more substan-tial places to live and trade – and this seems to have happened in Manchester. The Saxons had a profound effect on society during the time they were here, which incidentally was significantly longer than the Roman occupation, and left a legacy of laws, culture and place names that we can relate to even today.[4]

By around AD 900, the south-east Lancashire area became known as Salfordshire, and it seems that Manchester itself was nothing of significance at this stage.[5] Here, the Anglo-Saxons settled in the region and by the medieval period Manchester's former name of Mancunium had become Mamecester. Manchester was located on the border of the two Anglo-Saxon kingdoms of Northumbria and Mercia. It is known that around AD 923 Manchester was being governed by the kingdom of Northumbria, but this fell victim to an invasion of Danish tribes. Edward the Elder, the Saxon king of neighbouring Mercia, rescued and fortified Manchester and placed it under his command. Ancient manuscript evidence dating around the same time shows that a King Edward commanded the possession and reconstruction of 'Manchester in Northumbria' and occupied it.[6] It has been interpreted that it was the same Edward the Elder who was the son of Alfred the Great and who is likely to have rescued the area from the Danish invaders. However, attempts to keep the Danes at bay did not last for very long, since during the early part of the eleventh century Manchester came under the rule of the Danish King Canute, following his invasion of England in 1015. In 1031, Canute is believed to have visited Manchester whilst travelling north to encounter the Scots, and Knute Mill, which subsequently became Knott Mill, is thought to have been named after him. The Anglo-Saxons reclaimed the monarchy once more when Edward the Confessor came to power from 1042 until his death in 1066. Edward is known to have owned the land between the Rivers Ribble and Mersey in south-east Lancashire, and this territory became split into five districts, known as

Hundreds, of which Salford Hundred became the administrative district in which Manchester was located. The Saxons never left but their rule was taken away when the Normans invaded Britain.

The Manor of Manchester and Collegiate Church

When the Romans left the garrison at Castlefield the site was largely abandoned and the medieval centre began to emerge further upstream of the Rivers Irwell and Irk, on and around the present location of Manchester Cathedral at Hunt's Bank and Chetham's school and library. The buildings that form the Chetham's site today were originally the manor where the barons of Manchester governed. William the Conqueror, after his successful capture of the English throne from King Harold at the Battle of Hastings in 1066, began carving up land amongst his Norman knights. It was around the year 1075 that he gave all the land between the Rivers Ribble and Mersey in south-east Lancashire that was once owned by Edward the Confessor to Roger de Poitou. William Peverel, a son of William the Conqueror, inherited some of the estate of Roger de Poitou, including parts of the Salford Hundred, and he in turn gave some of these lands to Albert Gresley, who already held lands in the region, and these were extended to include much of the manor of Manchester. This marks the start of the Gresley dynasty as Lords of the Manor of Manchester, and during their rule, eight generations of the family occupied the manor, the first being Albert Gresley.[7] On Albert's death his son Robert became baron, and then the title was handed down to include Robert's son and grandson, both named Albert, and eventually a further Robert who became Lord of the Manor from 1182 until 1230. There is a little more information on this Robert Gresley, since his father died when he was a child and he had to be put under the guardianship of his mother and uncle until he came of age and was able to manage the manor himself.

Up to this point, none of the Lords of the Manor lived in Manchester, but the latter Robert was the first of the Gresley family to actually take up residence at Baron's Yard, and it is here that the manor and Manchester itself began to develop in size and status.[8] This Robert Gresley was certainly the first baron to put Manchester on the map, since it is under his rule that the medieval village starts to turn into an important regional commercial centre, since in 1222 and again in 1227, Robert obtained charters for annual fairs to be held in Manchester. Robert died around 1230 and his son Thomas took control of the manor. The next key figure in the Gresley dynasty was Thomas's grandson, another Thomas Gresley, who became Lord of the Manor in 1282, but, being only around 3 years of age, was under guardianship until he came of age. It is important to note this Thomas Gresley for his main achievements, since in 1301 he granted what became known as the *Great Charter* to the local inhabitants (or burgesses as they were known in medieval times). This was a highly important move for the region since it made Manchester a free borough with a number of important privileges.[9] To put the *Great Charter* into context, it largely upturned the feudal system (where a feudal lord held and exercised rights over the land and charged fees to tenants tied to the land in an agricultural economy) in which medieval manors were governed by enabling the locals to become free of this often restricted system, and most inhabitants became excluded from labour services that they were once tied into. In 1309, Thomas bequeathed the manor to his sister's husband, John de la Warre, since Thomas had not produced an heir. In 1313, Thomas died and John became Lord of the Manor, and here the manor passed into the family line of the de la Warres, the next important family in Manchester's history.

John de la Warre, the first of the de la Warre dynasty, became the ninth baron of Manchester.[10] John died around 1347 after a lengthy spell as Lord of the Manor and was succeeded by his grandson Roger de la Warre, since his son John had died before he could inherit the manor. Roger had two sons by his first marriage, John and Thomas, and a daughter Joan from his second marriage. Thomas went on to establish the Collegiate Church in 1421 and became its first rector. Roger's daughter Joan married Thomas West and one of their sons, Reginald West, eventually inherited the manor in 1427.

The history of the cathedral is very much connected to that of the manor. Whilst the site of the current cathedral dates from around 1215, when the large stone church was built, there is evidence that a Saxon church may have existed on this site, since an artefact known as the 'Angel Stone' was found embedded in the walls of the current cathedral that dates to around AD 700. However, since many buildings were constructed in part or wholly of timber at this time, this is the only piece of evidence that has been found that a church may have existed on the site before the one built in 1215. There is very little of the original medieval part of the building left in the current cathedral, as it has been renovated and rebuilt over the years and much of the building originates from the

Victorian era. Thomas de la Warre, as the first rector of the church, established the 'College' in 1421. So what was a 'college' at this time? By the early 1400s, it was decided that parish priests were not enough for the size of Manchester's ecclesiastical area, so Thomas petitioned both the Pope and the monarch of the day, King Henry V, to allow him to raise the church to that of collegiate status. Thomas indeed obtained a license from the king to establish the Collegiate Church, dedicated to St Mary, St Denys and St George. A college of priests was established in some new buildings close to the manor house. Thomas bequeathed around £3,000 in order to complete the college buildings, so existing buildings were demolished and the college was built, and an old local tale indicates that the new college was partially constructed from the remnants of the old buildings and stone from the Roman site at Castlefield. Unfortunately, there were insufficient funds to complete the project fully in stone, and parts of the buildings had to be constructed of wood. However, Thomas died in 1426, before he had chance to see his work completed, and it is not clear how much he had actually achieved before his death, though his legacy continued.

The Collegiate Church appointed a number of wardens over the years, all of whom made their mark on the building. John Huntington, the rector of Ashton-under-Lyne, was appointed as the first warden, together with eight priests, four clerks and six lay choristers. He was granted some land, and part of the manor. Huntington died in 1458 after thirty-seven years of dedicated service and was succeeded by John Booth, who became warden in 1459. However, Booth's tenure did not last nearly so long as his predecessor, since the role was taken from him in 1465 owing to the displeasure of Edward IV who not only stripped him of the role but fined him for his behaviour during the Wars of the Roses.[11] Ralph Langley replaced John Booth as the third warden of the Collegiate Church and he made a number of changes to the church, including construction of the nave during the 1460s and 1470s.[12] Subsequent wardens made structural alterations, and the fourth warden, John Stanley, former Bishop of Ely, altered some of this earlier work on the nave and also installed choir stalls.[13] Between 1421 and 1547 there were a total of seven wardens who looked after the college and church, all making changes and leaving their mark on the building.

Right 11 Plaque commemorating the role of Thomas de la Warre, outside Manchester Cathedral.

THOMAS de la WARRE

1350 – c.1426
RECTOR OF MANCHESTER
FOUNDED THE COLLEGIATE CHURCH IN 1421
WITH ITS COMMUNITY OF PRIESTS,
LAY CLERKS AND BOYS.

Below 12 Manchester Cathedral, formerly known as the Collegiate Church.

From Manorial Village to Trading Town

The story of how Manchester became a manor and important ecclesiastical area was largely determined by the monarchs and barons of the day, but what was everyday life like in medieval Manchester's town and economy? We now turn to trade and development of the town's urban structure. The trade that Manchester was engaging in was largely based around textiles, and the region became noted for this some centuries before it actually became famous for its industrial production of cotton. The local historian John Whitaker asserted that a form of woollen manufacture had been imported into Lancashire from France prior to the Roman arrival in Britain, and it continued during their occupation. It is indeed probable that the Romans introduced linen and hemp manufacture, though lack of real evidence unfortunately makes this claim unsubstantiated. It is clear that the Romans would have needed to produce clothing locally suitable for the north-west's climate, so the claim could well have some merits.[14] However, fulling mills (places where cloth was stretched out on frames and often located in water mills) were known to be in operation in the area, and there is evidence of woollen manufacture taking place in Ancoats from around the thirteenth century, but it is unclear how long these had been operating in the area.[15]

It was, in fact, events on the continental mainland that would provide the catalyst for trade in textile production in the region, as a number of Flemish linen weavers were known to have begun settling in the area from around the mid-thirteenth century.[16] During the fourteenth century, continental wars and the conditions they created in Flanders had become particularly harsh, and Flemish weavers were encourage to come to England by Edward III and Queen Philippa. As Philippa was also Flemish, it is thought that she was behind the decision to invite them to England. In particular, the conflict in Europe badly affected Flemish and French protestants, who were expelled from their respective countries and came to England to escape religious persecution. The Lord of the Manor at this time, John de la Warre, had been a former soldier in Flanders, and he also encouraged the weavers to settle in the region, not only to produce cloth but to teach locals vital skills of the textiles trade. The conflict that was negatively impacting on the European mainland proved to be an advantage for England, and in particular the north-west, in providing the ability to develop a thriving industrial economy, though England's island status was equally beneficial in that it was not touched by the European conflicts. This

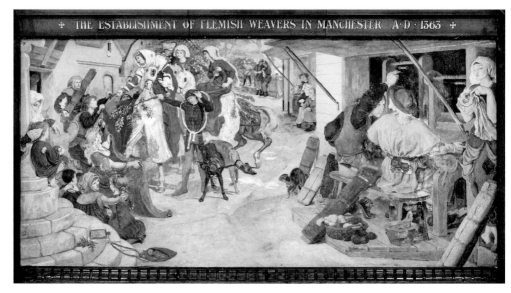

THE ESTABLISHMENT OF FLEMISH WEAVERS IN MANCHESTER · A·D· 1363

13 Ford Madox Brown, *The Establishment of the Flemish Weavers in Manchester.* (Courtesy of Manchester Libraries, Information and Archives, Manchester City Council)

allowed industry to thrive, and the skilled workforce could pass its abilities on to the locals. Many settled in Westmoreland, Lancashire and Yorkshire, and their fabrics became known as Kendal Cloth, Halifax Cloths and Manchester Cottons.[17] It is interesting to note that despite cotton being mentioned, much of the cloth produced at this time was woollen.

The arrival of the Flemish weavers was depicted in another of Ford Madox Brown's *Manchester Murals, The Establishment of the Flemish Weavers in Manchester*, which he completed in 1882, as one of the defining moments in Mancunian history, and illustrates a happy spring scene of the Flemish immigrants setting in the area and passing on their textiles skills and showing their cloth to Queen Philippa, who apparently made annual visits to the region. It is meant to convey an idyllic scene and it certainly contrasts quite markedly with the industrial production of cloth some centuries later. Here, Madox Brown reflects on the cotton industry of the nineteenth century and his painting recognises the start of the relationship with textiles in the region for which it became renowned. The historian John Mortimer, reflecting upon the painting, described the scene as 'the true starting point in the city's history as a place of manufacture and merchandise'.[18]

Trade and commerce in medieval Manchester also became visible through the weekly markets and an annual fair. In 1227, a second charter for an annual fair was granted by Henry III at the request of the third Baron of Manchester, Robert Gresley, and this lasted for up to three days. It initially took place in September but was later moved to October.[19] For a number of centuries the fair took place in Acresfield, which is the site of modern-day St Ann's Square. Acresfield was about 6.5 acres in area, and covered part of the original St Mary's churchyard. There are two theories as to how Acresfield it received its name. The first refers to 'Aca', who was a priest to whom Robert Gresley donated a piece of land around 1200, though the historian John Harland asserted that it was named after the Anglo-Saxon term for 'field'. The main forms of sale were farm animals and horses, and the animals were led from Deansgate through a narrow lane that became known as Toll Lane to the site of the fair. The lane was eventually developed and became St Ann's Street in the nineteenth century.[20] Manchester's enhanced status in becoming a market town was important because it meant that another market could not be held within a 6-mile radius, thus securing its position as a key trading centre in the region, and in 1359 Manchester was officially recognised as a market town. Market day was Saturday and traders from the local countryside would come in to sell their produce and here they paid a toll to the Lord of the Manor, which financed the growing town centre. There were a number of key streets that formed part of the market area of medieval Manchester, including Smithy Door, the road that led up to the Market Place. The area around the Market Place was notoriously difficult to keep clean, particularly with all the horses and farm animals that became a feature of trading life. The market grew in status and became a popular meeting place, and the community in the surrounding area also grew in size. Market traders were arranged in an orderly fashion and trades were located according to their type, where, for example, coopers and woodworkers were in a separate location from fruiterers. Butchers were all located near the Shambles; and Smithy Door was noted for its fish market from around the mid-sixteenth century.[21]

Manchester was governed by the Court Leet, which was the body that managed the medieval town, and here the Lord of the Manor could exercise certain rights over his tenants and deal with issues relating to land, but it also served as a way of maintaining social control and dealt with criminal offences. Records for the Manor of Manchester are available from the first recorded meeting that took place in 1552.[22] However, the Court Leet did exist prior to this, since it was the key form of medieval government in England. Records for Manchester during the 1550s indicate how the Court Leet was an integral part of town life and was a force for law and order and the upkeep of the town.[23] The records provide invaluable insights in to everyday life, and one example from the sixteenth century describes the concern the authorities had with the upkeep and cleanliness of the area, and so in 1570 Elizabeth Graye and Margaret Renshaye were appointed to keep Market Place clean, which they did on Tuesdays and Saturdays. It is these kinds of records that allow us to see how ordinary people lived and worked and how Manchester was developing as a market town. There are also glimpses into the management of local law and order and it is on record how some crimes were often punished by the stocks which were erected in the Market Place, and these were in operation from 1569 until 1816.[24] Court Leet sessions, under the jurisdiction of the Lord of the Manor, met twice a year, at Easter and Michaelmass. Here, the Boroughreeve (the chief officer of a town) and other officials of the manor were appointed, and these managed the town in dealing with issues on a day-to-day basis. The Boroughreeve and constables were usually people of status, such as merchants and businessmen, who lived in the local area and took the role for a year. There were other separate officers looking after different aspects of local administration such as taxes, weights and measures, and food inspection.[25] There was also a Court Baron for the recovery of debts and damages under 40 shillings, which was held every third Wednesday of the month.

The centre of medieval Manchester contained a small number of key streets which emanated from the manor, church and Market Place area, and the boundaries were confined to Hanging Bridge, Todd Street, Shudehill and Withy Grove. Streets were narrow, winding and unpaved, and in many respects regarded as 'a formless jumble of buildings', reflecting their early origins and lack of town planning.[26] Long Millgate, Deansgate, St Mary's Gate and Aldport Lane were all developing highways. Smithy Bank was suitably named after a blacksmith who erected a forge near the botton of Deansgate and the banks of the River Irwell. The street leading to the Baron's Mill near the manor house was known as Millgate, and when the mill was moved the roads close to where it was located became Long Millgate and Old Millgate. By 1282, there were an estimated 150 inhabitants, with a Court Leet to govern the growing area. Written records from around the sixteenth century provide a better understanding of what Manchester looked like and how it was growing, and accounts such as that provided by John Leland, who, as we have already seen, provided a description of Roman Manchester, enable us to picture the scene. Leland described Manchester in the 1530s as 'the fairest, best built, quickest and most populous town in all Lancashire, yet it is in it but one parish church', indicating that it was a small town but one of rapidly growing importance.[27]

The erection of the manor was followed by the construction of a water mill close by the Rivers Irk and Irwell between Smithy Door and Old Millgate. Communication between the manor, church and the mill was by Hanging Bridge, which covered Hanging Ditch. Even today, traces of Hanging Ditch and Hanging Bridge can still be found under the cathedral visitors centre on Cateaton Street. The first mention of Hanging Ditch was in 1316 when it was referred to in a property agreement but its age beyond this is uncertain. The first known reference to the bridge was later, in 1343, and it is referred to as *Hengand Brigge* in some property deeds, but it can only be assumed that it was there in 1316 when the ditch was previously mentioned. However, the ditch became rather a rubbish dump and sewer despite constant attempts to keep it clear, and eventually the river stopped flowing through it. It eventually became lost as buildings were constructed over the top and was only found again in the Victorian period after some basic excavations. In modern times it has been fully excavated and restored. Figures 14 and 15 show Hanging Bridge today and clearly show the route to the cathedral, and underneath are the bridge arches and parts of the ditch, which can be accessed through the cathedral visitors centre. Other nearby key roads that were developing include Shudehill and Withy Grove. The first mention of Shudehill was in 1554 but it is thought to be older. Withy Grove was formerly known as 'Withingreave' and is described in the 1560s as a country lane. In 1569, Roger Bexwicke became a land tenant here and paid 8 shillings to the Lord of the Manor. There was an old inn on Withy Grove, the Seven Stars Inn, and Withingreave Hall once stood near the junction with Shudehill.[28]

Further afield, modern-day Piccadilly was known as Lever's Row and contained Daub Holes, which were large ponds and a notable feature of the area. Lever's Hall was a black-and-white Tudor-style building which housed the Lever family, of which Sir Ashton Lever was the best known. The White Bear Inn in Piccadilly was built on the original site of Lever's Hall and was one of the area's main coaching inns during the latter stages of the eighteenth and nineteenth centuries.[29] Lever's Row was renamed as Piccadilly in 1812 at the same time that Market Stead Lane became Market Street. The existence of Daub Holes is well known through references in local Court Leet records. Daub was a type of clay extensively used in medieval and early modern buildings, which would often be sourced locally. The large dimples that were created by mining

14 Hanging Bridge today.

15 Rear of Hanging Bridge and the former ditch that now forms part of the cathedral visitors centre.

clay filled with water, producing large ponds. Close to Daub Holes was Garrett Lane, which in modern times became Portland Street. It was the location of Garrett Hall, another black-and-white Tudor-style mansion. It is known that during the fourteenth century it was occupied by the Traffords, and it remained in the family until the death of Ralph Trafford around 1555. Court Leet records indicate that there were a number of possible contenders to inherit the hall but it appears that Gilbert Gerard acquired the estate. In 1596, it was sold by the Gerard family to Oswald Mosley. Oswald's son Samuel sold the hall to Ralph Hough in 1631.[30] The hall was still in existence into the nineteenth century but by this time had started to decay and eventually disappeared. Slightly further afield was Radclifte Hall, which was located around Pool Fold, a small street close to Cross Street, and here was located the ducking stool that was used to chastise gossiping women, until it was relocated to Daub Holes during the seventeenth century. Fountain Street, parallel with Cross Street, was, as its name implies, where water could be accessed, and not far from Spring Gardens, which was also a local source of water. It is believed that around 1550 Isabel Beck, a wealthy local widow, ensured that a source of water was piped from here to the Market Place.[31]

Like Roman Manchester, medieval Manchester was shaped by its rivers, particularly around the Collegiate Church where the rivers flowing nearby were crossed by several bridges. One of the main bridges was Salford Bridge, which crossed the River Irwell at the bottom of Cateaton Street. It was located close to the Collegiate Church and was very old indeed, its earliest reference being in 1368 where it was mentioned in the will of Thomas del Bothe of Eccles who donated £30 to the bridge for its upkeep. During the reign of Edward III a chapel was built on the bridge and here travellers could offer thanks for safe passage. This chapel was rebuilt in 1505, but fell into decay once more and in 1573 the chapel closed and the structure became the local prison until 1776, when it was finally taken down.[32] The prison had two cells and it believed that those incarcerated in the lower cell were particularly unlucky since they faced problems with the river flooding without any hope of escaping.[33] Anyone caught drunk spent the night there and had to pay sixpence to the poor, and if they could not afford to pay up, the publican whose hostelry had contributed to their inebriated state had to pay for them. In 1642 during the Civil War, the Royalists under command of Lord Strange began the siege of Manchester and unsuccessfully tried to enter Manchester via the bridge, and this will be explored in the next chapter.[34] The River Irk could be crossed nearby by one of four bridges, one close to Hunt's Bank, a second at the end of Toad Lane (later Mill Brow), a third towards the end of Milner's Lane (later Miller Street), and a fourth near Long Millgate to Red Bank. Manchester was also being divided into different districts, and in addition to Castlefield there were also the areas of Camp Field, Dole Field and Parsonage Field. During the thirteenth century the name Alport began appearing in records, meaning 'old town', and referred to the area slightly east of the former Roman garrison at Castlefield. The wider area also contained the hamlets of Ancoats and Collyhurst. Other areas that we are familiar today with in and around Manchester were in evidence during medieval times, and here there were Salford, Cheetham, Newton, Ardwick, Chorlton Row, Stretford, Withington, Rusholme, and Gorton, all under the direction of a lord with surrounding lands used for cultivation.[35]

Conclusion

Between the Roman departure and the Norman Conquest, Manchester's history is relative obscurity and, whilst there are theories and legends, there is little evidence to tell us a great deal about the area at this time. However, medieval Manchester, from the time of William the Conqueror, emerged from manorial village to an aspiring trading town that began to take shape as an area for commerce and textile production and it is in the fourteenth century that we see textiles as a key trade begin to mark Manchester out for specialisation in this aspect of the economy. The town itself developed around the Collegiate Church and manor, with the streets around Market Place becoming a trading focal point. The Gresleys, followed by the de la Warres, were significant families that governed the area, and their legacy was felt in the creation of the ecclesiastical college. The *Great Charter* allowed the development of markets and fairs that opened up Manchester to trade and commerce and in many respects managed the economy not so much as a form of feudalism but as a market economy, and arguably this enabled Manchester to lay the foundations of the trade and commerce that was to come. The Flemish weavers were instrumental in taking the textiles trade forwards, and the next chapter takes the story of trade towards the modern era.

Notes

1 Hollingworth, R., *Mancuniensis, or a History of the Towne of Manchester*, 1839 (1656), pp. 21–22.
2 Axon, W., *The Annals of Manchester*, John Heywood, 1885, p. v.
3 *The Ancient Ballad of Tarquin* was reprinted in 1808 by J. Aston.
4 Harland, J., *Mamecestre* vol. 1, vol. LIII, Chetham's Society Publications, 1861.
5 Axon, *The Annals of Manchester*, p. 5.
6 Harland, *Mamecestre* vol. 1, Chetham's Society Publications; see also Baines, E., *History of the County Palatine of Lancaster*, George Routledge & Sons, 1868., vol. 1, p. 52.
7 See Tait, J., *Medieval Manchester and the Beginnings of Lancashire* (Sherratt & Hughes, 1904) for more information on the Gresley dynasty.
8 Harland, Mamecestre, vol. 1, pp. 23–37.
9 Parkinson-Bailey, J., *Manchester: An Architectural History*, Manchester University Press, 2000, ch. 1.
10 Aikin, J., A *Description of the Country from Thirty to Forty Miles Around Manchester*, 1795, p. 148.

11 Hibbert Ware, S., *History of the Foundation in Manchester of Christ's College, Chetham's Hospital and the Free Grammar School*, vol. 1, Thomas Agnew & Joseph Zanetti, 1830, ch. 1.

12 Hibbert Ware, *History of the Foundation*, ch. 1.

13 Parkinson-Bailey, *Manchester*, ch. 1.

14 Harland, J., *Collectanea Relating to Manchester and its Neighbourhood*, vol. 1, Chetham Society, 1866., p. 24.

15 Axon, *The Annals of Manchester*, p. vi.

16 Mortimer, J., *Mercantile Manchester: past and present*, Palmer Howe, 1896, p. 1.

17 Hibbert Ware, *History of the Foundation*, p. 21.

18 Mortimer, *Mercantile Manchester*, p. 1.

19 Axon, *The Annals of Manchester*, p. 10.

20 Swindells, *Manchester Streets*, vol. 1, p. 85.

21 Swindells, *Manchester Streets*, vol. 3, pp. 131–4.

22 Axon, *Annals of Manchester*, p. 28.

23 'Townships: Manchester (part 2 of 2)', in *A History of the County of Lancaster*: vol. 4, ed. William Farrer and J. Brownbill (London, 1911), pp. 230–51. British History Online http://www.british-history.ac.uk/vch/lancs/vol.4/pp230-251 [accessed 5 September 2016].

24 Swindells, *Manchester Streets*, vol. 3, p. 133–40.

25 Simon, S., *A Century of City Government*, p. 39.

26 Kidd, A., *Manchester*, Edinburgh University Press, 2002, p. 32.

27 Swindells, *Manchester Streets*, vol. 4, p.3.

28 Swindells, *Manchester Streets*, vol. 5, p. 84.

29 Parkinson-Bailey, *Manchester*, p. 7.

30 Swindells, *Manchester Streets*, vol. 2, pp. 1–3 & 60–5.

31 Swindells, *Manchester Streets*, vol. 3, p. 143.

32 Everett, J., *Panorama of Manchester and Railway Companion*, 1834, p. 21.

33 Hibbert Ware, *History of the Foundation*, ch. 1.

34 Swindells, *Manchester Streets*, vol. 1, p. 34.

35 Everett, *Panorama of Manchester*, p. 12.

three

PRECURSOR TO A REVOLUTION

Mamcestre ... is the fairest, best buildied, quikkest and most populus tounne of al Lancastreshire.

John Leland (1538)

Introduction

So far, Manchester has emerged from a Roman garrison to a manor town that was rapidly developing into an important commercial and trading centre, with an infrastructure that was progressing ahead of its time. During this phase, from around the 1550s to the 1780s, this process continued, while textiles became firmly rooted in the local economy and Manchester was the central point in a network of trade and commerce for surrounding towns and villages. This is also a time where a number of key institutions emerge, such as the Grammar School, Chetham's Library, and public institutions such as prisons. The people of Manchester were also confronted with a number of political and religious issues, the first of which was the Civil War in the 1640s with the siege of Manchester in 1642 emphasising support for the Parliamentarians who opposed the Royalists under the command of Charles I, and the politics that followed this with differing allegiances to the monarchy and Stuart dynasty that were shaping politics at both national and local levels. During the latter part of the period, radical political allegiances were forming that would continue to have ramification in later centuries, both in terms of Jacobitism in supporting the Stuart monarchy, and of Jacobinism that supported the 'Church and King' against revolutionary radical threats that emanated from the French Revolution at the close of the eighteenth century. Many of the political debates took place in local inns that were known for following particular political allegiances, and this would play out over the course of the eighteenth century and into the early part of the nineteenth century. This time was a precursor to a revolution, in both industrial and social terms.

Urban Development

Manchester's population was increasing, and it has been estimated that in 1588 there were around 10,000 inhabitants, rising to around 20,000 by the mid-1700s, and by 1773 just over 22,000 people lived in Manchester.[1] Some of these figures are estimates, though in 1773 there was a survey of the local population that allows for a more accurate estimation. Manchester did not escape the plague that had devastated many parts of the country and in some respects was modestly affected compared to other regions, when in 1605 around 1,000 deaths were reported.[2] By the 1650s the centre had grown to comprise of around fifteen main streets including Market Place, Market Stead Lane, Deansgate, Smithy Door, Withy Grove, Shudehill, Fennel Street, and Hunt's Bank. The centre was about a mile wide and, as with many medieval and early modern towns, many of the buildings were irregular black-and-white constructions, often with smaller courtyards running off in a warren of ill-planned spaces. Close to Long Millgate was the Old Apple Market, and Fennel Street housed the Hay Market. Close to Market Place was 'Booths', which was the municipal building that looked after the administration of the manor, and here the Court Leet and other court proceedings were held. The pillory, stocks and whipping post for miscreants remained in the Market Place close to the fish market, so the court and dispensing of punishments were conveniently close together. Market Stead Lane had expanded and comprised higher status shops, often run by tradesmen and merchants in the textiles and leather trades. Manchester had become home to four market places and continued to hold two market days, on Tuesday and Saturday. By the 1600s, there were three fairs each year, the Easter Knott Mill Fair, Acres Fair, and a Whitsuntide Fair in nearby Salford.[3] Despite the town growing, there were problems that were holding back the region's commercial activity, and this included the poor transport infrastructure. Transport by road and river was a particular problem, with roads that were heavily reliant on pack horses as the main vehicles, and rivers that were not always navigable.[4] Like many towns and villages, a number of inns had opened around the centre and were offering sociability, accommodation and stabling for commercial travellers. For example, on the other side of the Collegiate Church were the Blackamoor's Head and Ring o' Bells public houses. The Wellington Inn, which is still in existence, is a medieval inn that, despite having been modified over the centuries and even physically moved in the wake of the IRA bombing of Manchester in 1996, is still a close representation of its original architectural style. Its narrow construction with three floors, low beams and small mullion windows are representative of its early origins. The Sun Inn was another of Manchester's old inns, which unfortunately has not survived. Its style of architecture very much reflected the medieval style of black-and-white beams and irregular construction. During the nineteenth century, it was often referred to as 'Poet's Corner' where the likes of the radical poet Samuel Bamford and other literary specialists often met to recite their works.[5] The Seven Stars, located on Withy Grove, has been considered to be one of Britain's oldest licensed premises, though it is difficult to verify this claim since establishments that sold ale did not require a license until the middle of the sixteenth century, but it does appear that the building itself dated to around the fourteenth century.[6] The Bull's Head Inn in Market Place was one of the most famous inns in central Manchester and was the focal point for a range of clubs, commercial activity and visits by dignitaries. It was a centre for both news and politics, and was noted for its Jacobite tendencies, where its clientele were prominent supporters of 'Church and King', and this is an issue that will be explored later.[7] Some of Manchester's inns had been former grand residences that had been turned into inns, and one such example was the Palace Inn on Market Street which had been a mansion and later became an inn that was a favourite for eminent travellers. During 1745, the Palace Inn, which at the time was managed by John Dickenson, was known to have entertained the Young Pretender, Bonny Prince Charlie.[8] The Manchester Arms, located in Long Millgate Collegiate Church district, was also a former grand residence and originally the home of the Haworth family.

The last chapter described the development of the college. From the middle of the sixteenth century it went through a number of changes. It was ironic that the college survived the onslaught of King Henry VIII during the Reformation and the religious turbulence this created across the country, but it unfortunately

16 The Old Wellington Inn.

did not survive his son Edward VI's intervention when he became king, since in 1547, under Edward's instruction, the college was dissolved and its buildings and lands were handed to the Earl of Derby, who employed around four ministers to maintain some basic church proceedings whilst it was in this dissolved state. In 1553, Edward VI died and his half-sister Mary Tudor became queen and she re-established the college. As part of this reinstatement, she requested that the former warden, George Collyer, return to the post he had once held. She also appointed a master, eight chaplains, four clerks and six choristers. When Elizabeth I became monarch, it was unclear what she would do with the college but she granted a new charter in 1578. In 1636, Charles I granted a fourth charter. However, it was during the Civil War under Charles I's reign that the status of the college changed, when the country was tipped into political and religious turmoil, and the college buildings were used to store munitions during the Civil War. In 1649 it was ransacked.

17 Gate at Chetham's.

18 Rear of Chetham's.

However, from around 1617, a local merchant, Humphrey Chetham, who would prove instrumental in the survival of the college, was already investing in the college buildings. Chetham was born in Crumpsall in 1580. His father was a successful merchant and Chetham followed in his footsteps. He attended the Manchester Grammar School and later took up employment with a draper, and this led him to a career as a merchant in the textiles trade. He spent much of his wealth in the college and its buildings, and used some of his wealth to create the Blue Coat School, which initially educated around forty boys, and a hospital. After Chetham's death in 1653, his bequest was used to buy the surrounding buildings, and the library was established. The library is regarded as one of the oldest English-speaking public libraries in the world, and is certainly the oldest public library in Britain, and continues to this day.

19 Chetham's Library.

The manor had passed from the de la Warres to the West family, from Reginal West who held the baronry from 1427 until 1579, and then William West, who sold the manor, with all its rights and privileges, to the London cloth worker, John Lacye, for £3,000. Lacye subsequently sold it to Nicholas Mosley in 1596 for £3,500. Mosley, despite being a native of Manchester, had lived in London for some time and even became Mayor of London, but the Mosley family had a textiles business and worked between the two cities. From this generation to the nineteenth century, the manor remained in the possession of the Mosley family.[9] Nicholas Mosley was the son of Edward Mosley of Hough End, Withington. He managed the London side of the family textile business, and was elected Lord Mayor of London in 1599 and also received a knighthood around the same time. Sir Nicholas retired in 1602 and returned to Manchester, residing at Hough End Hall in Chorlton-cum-Hardy. The family also acquired the manor of Cheetham and Cheetwood, and Nicholas' son, Rowland Mosley, paid £8,000 to Sir Robert Cecil for the manors of Withington and Hough.[10] In terms of the governance and administration of Manchester, the Mosley family remained in charge of the manor until the 1830s when Manchester town council bought the rights for £200,000 and the Mosleys remained Lord of the Manor until 1835.[11] By the 1830s, it was clear that Manchester needed a far more modern way of governing the town, and the role of the manor ended as a new form of managing the modern city was created.

There were some other key institutions emerging during the 1500s. In 1580, a new prison was built in Manchester at Hunt's Bank, called the 'New Fleet'. During Tudor times it was mainly used to house those who were facing religious persecution and who remained loyal to the Catholic Church. These prisoners had broken the law of the *Popish Recusants Act* of 1605. At the hands of the Bishop of Chester and the Earl of Derby, those recusants imprisoned in Chester were relocated to Manchester. At first these were held in Radcliff Hall, which was a secure building, but there was a need for more purpose-built premises. Previously, miscreants were incarcerated in the former chapel on Salford Bridge, but there was a need for a proper prison building as the population increased. Later, New Fleet prison housed prisoners who had committed all kinds of offences. Funding the New Fleet was achieved by fining wealthier prisoners and by the proceeds of a parochial assessment, which amounted to 8 pence each week on every parish through the Diocese of Chester.[12] New Fleet prison lasted until around 1774 but was eventually replaced and a new prison, the New Bailey, was complete in 1790.

In 1515, the Free Grammar School was founded by Hugh OIdham, the Bishop of Exeter, which today is the Manchester Grammar School. Bishop Oldham died in 1519 and did not live to see the first school building, which was completed in 1520 in Long Millgate, close by the present entrance to the Chetham's complex. The school was financed through income from the manor's mills, and the Court Leet was eager to remind locals that if they stopped using the mills it would lead to the school not being financed and could close. In the rules governing the school, it was stated that no scholar, regardless of background or wherever they came from, would be refused admission.[13] It was originally called the Manchester School and came with land and a lease which was purchased for sixty years. It began with two teachers but by the 1830s this had risen to five. All the pupils were boys and, by the 1830s, comprised both boarders and day attenders.[14] The grammar school indeed not only survived but thrived and moved to new premises in Fallowfield in 1931. It is still at this latter site today, and has an impressive reputation for education.[15]

Trade and Commerce

The sixteenth-century historian William Cambden described Elizabethan Manchester as:

> Far excelling the towns about it for the beautiful shew it carrieth and for resort to it
> ... in the last age much more famous for its manufacture of stuffs called Manchester
> cottons.[16]

Whilst Manchester has always been associated with cotton, it was in fact wool and linen that were used more widely at this time and preceded the cotton for which Manchester ultimately became famous.[17] Cloth production was very much a domestic industry with separate specialisms in spinning and weaving, where Manchester became the commercial centre of a network of rural villages that were producing thread and cloth for sale, and where merchants were engaged in trade and distribution.[18] It has already been shown how textiles had developed into a prominent part of the local economy, and it was growing at a rapid rate between the sixteenth and eighteenth centuries. In addition to the Flemish textile workers who came to settle in the region during the medieval period, further persecution of Protestants in Flanders led to even more continental textiles workers arriving in Britain by the mid-sixteenth century, so by this time the Manchester region had inherited a highly skilled workforce who were creating a thriving woollen cloth trade.[19] There is evidence of how cloth production was important to Manchester's economy, since, for example, in 1524 there is a record of one Martin Brian, a woollen cloth maker living in Manchester, and in 1541 an Act of Parliament refers to the town as 'well inhabited for a long time, and the King's subjects well set a work in the making of clothes as well of linen as of woollen'.[20] By 1552, an Act of Parliament stated that 'all cottons called Manchester, Lancashire and Cheshire cottons shall be in length 22 yards, and that all Manchester rugs otherwise Manchester frizes shall contain in length 36 yards'. By 1565, 'aulnegers', or parliamentary agents, were stationed at Manchester for stamping woollen cloth.[21] The historian Thomas Swindells, in his descriptions of Manchester, mentions John May, who in 1613 published a pamphlet making reference to both Manchester cottons and fustian (a thick cloth of cotton and linen which sometimes included wool), which were purchased in lengths called a 'kersie'.[22] There is evidence that there was trade in cotton with Cyprus and Turkey by the mid-seventeenth century, since the British merchant and writer, Lewis Roberts, in 1641 published a pamphlet on foreign trade, indicating a thriving overseas trade of buying and selling, in which he states:[23]

> The town of Manchester in Lancashire must be remembered, and worthily for their encouragement commended, who buy the yarn of the Irish in great quantity, and weaving it, return the same again in linen into Ireland to sell. Neither doth the industry rest here, for they buy cotton wool in London that comes first from Cyprus and Smyrna, and at home work the same and perfect it in fustians, vermillions, dymities and other such stuffs, and then return it to London, where the same is vented and sold, and not seldom sent into foreign parts, which have means, at far easier terms, to provide themselves of the paid first materials.[24]

It can be confusing for us today to understand how woollen cloth was known as Manchester cottons, and consequently it can be difficult to pin down exactly when these Manchester cottons became actual cotton, though Lewis Roberts, in 1641, seemed to suggest that cotton did in fact mean cotton by this time.[25] It was around the 1650s that 'chapmen' appeared, whose role was to purchase grey cloth and finish it for resale. Humphrey Chetham undertook such a role as a principal cloth buyer in Bolton and where he accumulated much wealth as a result.[26] The Mosley family continued to engage in the textiles trade operating between Manchester and London from the late sixteenth and early seventeenth centuries. Nicholas Mosley spent much of his time in London operating the southern end of the family business, and brothers Oswald and Anthony remained in Manchester. By the end of the sixteenth century, Manchester had grown into a key marketing and regional centre for trade and commerce in wool and linen, with strong connections to London for trade with the continent, the West Riding of Yorkshire, and via the ports of Chester and Liverpool to trade with Ireland'.[27] Historian William Axon, in his *Annals of Manchester*, recalls Manchester and Salford in 1650:

> The people in and about the town are said to be in general the most industrious in their callings of any in the northern parts of the kingdom. The town is a mile in length, the streets open and clean kept, and the buildings good. The trade is not inferior to that of many cities in the kingdom, chiefly consisting in woollen friezes, fustians, sackcloths, mingled stuffs, caps, inkles, tapes, points etc, whereby not only the better sort of men are employed, but also the very children by their own labour can maintain themselves; there are besides all kinds of foreign merchandise brought and returned by the merchants of the town, amounting to the sum of many thousands of pounds weekly.[28]

Religion and Politics

The early modern era was a time of religious and political turbulence. This was witnessed across Britain but certainly around Manchester, and the region was at the heart of religious and political divisions. It is necessary to explain events at national level in order to understand local politics. In 1603, the last of the Tudors, Elizabeth I, died without an heir and the throne went to the Stuarts of Scotland, with James I, son of Mary Queen of Scots, becoming king of both Scotland and England. Britain at this time was a religiously divided place, with Catholics pitched against Protestants, and this was largely driven by the religious stance of the monarchy. The death of Elizabeth I not only symbolised the end of the Tudors but the crown changed from Protestantism to Catholicism. Catholics had faced persecution under the latter part of Elizabeth's reign, and despite James I promising that the same fate would not happen to Protestants under his reign, he did not keep his word. So, people either liked him or loathed him and there was little middle ground. The effects of James's reign were very much felt in the region, and he had support from prominent Lancashire families, including the Hoghtons of Hoghton Hall near Preston. He was succeeded by his son Charles I in 1625, and his reign was much more problematic than that of his father. Charles I very much believed in the divine rights of kings, whose rule must not be challenged, and this led him into conflict with Parliament, which was far from happy with this overbearing approach from a monarch that refused to listen to reason. Such was the dispute between the monarchy and Parliament that civil war broke out, dividing not only the country but often families who had differing views on how the country should be ruled. This war, which lasted around seven years, ended when Charles I was beheaded in Whitehall in 1649. The execution of the monarch meant Britain became a republic under the leadership of Oliver Cromwell from 1649 to 1660 in what is known as the Interregnum. It certainly did not mark immediate peace, and the aftershock of the monarch's death resulted in several decades of political and religious uncertainty. It did not help that Cromwell's son was not as politically shrewd as his father, and in 1660 the monarchy was restored with Charles II, who had made a number of promises in order to regain the crown for his family. Manchester did not escape the Civil War that affected much of England during the 1640s. Despite some Royalist sympathies, Manchester was a largely Parliamentarian area, and supported Oliver Cromwell against the monarchy and Charles I. In July 1642, the Civil War came to the centre of Manchester, which resulted in a week-long siege when the Royalists attempted to gain the town back to their control and to promote support for the king. The Earl of Derby was one of the most powerful men in Lancashire and a firm Royalist, and in case of conflict had munitions stashed away in key northern towns, including Manchester. The munitions here were stored in the Collegiate Church, and Charles I ordered their retrieval. In 1642, attempts were made to remove them, but unfortunately for the Royalists, local Parliamentarians had beaten them to it and already removed the stash. Even a local militia was formed in anticipation of Royalist trouble. Predictably, Charles I wanted his gunpowder, and by now the Earl of Derby's son, Lord Strange, had taken up the mantle of his father. Here, he helped his old friend Charles I by mustering a military force and set out for Manchester. In a siege that lasted for around seven days, one of the Royalist attacks came via Salford Bridge. However, the Parliamentarians were prepared and the defensive positions of Captains Rosworm, Bradshaw and Booth were too much for Lord Strange's men. Strange even tried to call a

20 Ford Madox Brown, *Bradshaw's Defence of Manchester*. (Courtesy of Manchester Libraries, Information and Archives, Manchester City Council)

ceasefire and negotiate terms but this was refused and the fighting continued. Four days into the siege it was announced in the House of Commons that 'the beginning of Civil Warres in England: or terrible news from the North'.[29] The siege took place around the college and the former manor was taken over as a prison and stores for weapons. The Parliamentarians won the day and the Royalists under Lord Strange retreated. The following year, in January 1643, Sir Thomas Fairfax made Manchester the headquarters for the Parliamentary army for the region.[30] The siege of Manchester has been memorably captured in one of the Ford Madox Brown's *Manchester Murals*, *Bradshaw's Defence of Manchester*. In fact, the scene is not so much triumphalism but illustrates how difficult the battle became in retaining Manchester as a Parliamentarian stronghold while the battle ensued on Salford Bridge.

The restoration of the monarchy under Charles II resulted in further religious and political uncertainty. In 1662, the *Act of Uniformity* attempted to impost state-based controls on the style of worship in the Church of England. One of the symbols that epitomises this religious uncertainty in Manchester is Cross Street Chapel. Originally, it was a Dissenters meeting house and a nonconformist church and was established following the *Act of Uniformity* in 1662, when many preachers rejected this imposition. The Reverend Henry Newcome, a former preacher of the Collegiate Church, formed his own congregation of

21 Cross Street Chapel, *c.* 1879. (Copyright University of Manchester)

followers as he was unable to retain his position at the church following the restoration of the monarchy. The Dissenters Meeting House was opened in 1664, where he led congregations from 1664 until his death in 1695. A purpose-built church that became Cross Street Chapel held it first religious service in June 1694.[31] Cross Street Chapel became a Unitarian place of worship in 1761. Cross Street Chapel was not the only place of worship built during this period that reflected a diversity of religious views. Lady Ann Bland, the daughter of Sir Edward Mosley, and Lady of the Manor, had been a follower of Henry Newcome, and after his death she felt that a church had to be established that was a proper alternative to the Collegiate Church in what became known as 'High Church' versus 'Low Church', at a time where religion and politics became both mixed together and complicated. Lady Ann was very much of the 'Low Church' tradition of worship as a Presbyterian. The Collegiate Church had become associated with the Tory party and St Ann's Church became associated with the Whig political tradition. The construction of St Ann's Church by Lady Ann Bland provided the alternative means of worship for those who supported the 'Low Church'. This was also reflected in the public houses in the

22 Cross Street Chapel in the twenty-first century.

23 St Ann's Church in St Ann's Square, formerly Acresfield.

area. The Bull's Head Inn became a Tory stronghold of 'Church and King' men and the Angel public house in Market Stead Lane was a Whig stronghold.[32] In 1708, an act was passed to build St Ann's Church on Acresfield, the site of the old fair. The foundation stone was laid by Lady Ann in 1709 and in July 1712 the church was consecrated by the Bishop of Chester.[33] The first rector was Reverend Nathaniel Bann.[34] In 1777, parts of the original tower became dangerous and were taken down and replaced by a spire, but soon afterwards this was again replaced by a new tower.[35] Figure 23 shows the church today, one of Manchester's most beautiful buildings.

Eighteenth-Century Politics: Jacobitism and Jacobinism

Manchester had become a politically and religiously divided place, certainly vocal, some would conclude even revolutionary. There were two movements that were prevalent in eighteenth-century Manchester that are often confused but were very distinct in their ideologies. Jacobitism related to the following of the Stuart monarchy, and Jacobinism was a revolutionary movement that stemmed from the French Revolution of 1789. The first of these, Jacobitism, was prevalent from the turn of the eighteenth century, the aim of which was to restore the Catholic James II of England to the throne, following him being deposed in 1688 and replaced by his daughter and son-in-law Mary II and William III of Orange. The Stuarts lived in exile, but made several attempts to regain the crown. There were some key areas of support for the Stuarts, notably parts of Scotland, Ireland, Wales and south-west England, and areas of Northern England, particularly around Northumberland and Lancashire. There were many Stuart sympathisers in the Manchester area, and this spilled over into the 1715 uprising, when the clergy sided with James II's son, James Edward (also known as the Old Pretender). On the death of Queen Anne in 1714, George I came to the throne and Jacobites were furious, claiming that the rightful heir was the son of James II, and the dispute between the two sides resulted in a rebellion that affected many northern towns. Tensions in Manchester erupted in May 1715, when many were proclaiming James Edward Stuart as king.[36] On 10 June 1715, local Jacobites under the lead of local black-smith Tom Syddall began rioting and caused damage to a number of houses, but the most badly affected building was the Dissenting chapel on Cross Street. Syddall and his fellow conspirators were subsequently convicted at Lancaster

24 Plaque on a building in Byrom Street showing the place where Charles Edward Stuart stored guns as part of the Jacobite uprising of 1745.

Assizes and imprisoned at Lancaster Castle, but released by the army of the Jacobite rebellion. He joined forces with them but was taken prisoner again at Preston. He was tried again, this time at Liverpool, and was sent for the death penalty with five other rebels. Syddall was executed on 11 February 1716, and his head was fixed on the Market Cross in the centre of Manchester as an example to those that might consider similar action. In the wake of the trial at Liverpool and Syddall's execution, thirty-four others were also executed at various places around Lancashire.[37] Parliament granted around £1,500 to restore Cross Street Chapel, which reopened in the spring of 1716. Some thirty years later, in 1745, rebellion broke out again. This time it was Charles Edward Stuart (or Bonny Prince Charlie, the 'Young Pretender') who attempted to secure the British crown for the exiled Stuarts. He began to gather troops en route from Scotland through Carlisle and Lancashire towards Manchester. Here, around 300 joined his Jacobite entourage in what eventually became known as the Manchester Regiment, which was placed under the command of Colonel

Francis Townley.[38] The regiment reached as far as Carlisle but had to retreat and surrender. During his stay in Manchester, Bonnie Prince Charlie stayed at the Palace Inn and it is believed that the name of the inn reflected this visit and became a favourite destination for eminent travellers.[39]

Jacobinism was another ideological force that was prominent during this period and this stemmed from the political and religious differences that followed on from the Civil War. Later in the eighteenth century, these were to surface once more. However, the influence this time was political events in continental Europe, where the French Revolution in 1789 caused ripples of political discontent across the continent, and again it was a rebellion against the divine rule of monarchs, who utterly abused their power and wealth whilst ordinary people suffered poverty and starvation. The French Revolution demonstrated that collectively people can come together to change the political system and overturn their oppressors. This was keenly felt in the region where the Church, monarchy and the State in England were seen to oppose reform that would allow ordinary people to have a political voice and better living conditions. A 'Church and King' Club was formed in Manchester, whose base was the Bull's Head Inn, and its members partook in a number of rituals and symbolism such as their dress, and in meetings had toasts declaring 'Church and King and down with the Rump', the Rump being an illegitimate parliament, as they saw it. Counter-clubs were formed, including the Manchester Constitutional Society. The local press, voices of political opinion, were very much on the side of the Church and seen to oppose liberty and justice. Here, the *Wheeler's Manchester Chronicle* and the *Manchester Mercury* were very much of the 'High Church' tradition, and to counteract this another paper, in the form of the *Manchester Herald*, was created to provide a voice for liberal values, though it did not last, as it was created in 1792 but was effectively put down in March 1793. In local taverns, boards were put up in stating 'no Jacobins admitted here' starting a trend of attempting to prevent political discussion in public houses. Publicans were often threatened with their licenses if they held meetings of clubs such as the Manchester Constitutional Society. Here is what 186 Manchester publicans signed up to:

Manchester, September 13, 1792

We, whose names are hereunto subscribed, being licensed innkeepers and ale-housekeepers, within the towns of Manchester and Salford, justly alarmed at the treasonable and seditious conduct of a well-known set of daring miscreants, who dare called a public meeting to be held on Tuesday next, at the Bull's Head Inn, in Manchester, for the avowed purpose of assisting the French savages, as well as with a sincere desire of introducing similar calamities to the inhabitants of this happy and prosperous Country, as those that now exist in France, take this very necessary opportunity of publishing to the towns of Manchester and Salford in particular, and to the whole kingdom of Great Britain in general our detestation of such wicked and abominable practices. And we do hereby solemnly declare, that we will not suffer any meeting to be held in our houses of any CLUB or societies, however specious or plausible their titles may be that have a tendency to put in force what those INTERNALS so ardently and devoutly wish for, namely, the destruction of this country ; and we will be ready on all occasions to co-operate with our fellow-townsmen in bringing to justice all those who shall offend in any instance against our much admired and most excellent constitution.[40]

It is here that a radical political tradition in Manchester emerged as the Industrial Revolution began and the divisions about the political rights of ordinary working people who were without a political voice were becoming prominent in local society. The effects of the French Revolution were very much present in Manchester and there was revolution in the air, much to the alarm of those with all the power.

Conclusion

This chapter has revealed how Manchester had developed just prior to the Industrial Revolution, where its infrastructure had developed and the textiles industry was the key form of the local economy. It was also a time of turbulence and rebellion when politics and religion met, often with violent results, and national politics was certainly felt locally as the Civil War came to town and Protestantism was conflicting with Catholicism and monarchy conflicting with Parliamentarians. Political and religious factions could be seen even in local inns, such was the divisive nature of the issues of the time. The story now moves on to consider the early part of the Industrial Revolution as the economic and social impact took hold on the region and left an indelible mark on Manchester, in terms of both the factories that sprung up and also the dreadful conditions local people endured.

Notes

1 Aikin, J., *A Description of the Country from Thirty to Forty Miles Around Manchester* (1795), p. 156; Everett, J., *Panorama of Manchester and Railway Companion* (1834), pp. 41–2.

2 *Court Leet Records for the Manor of Manchester*, vol. VI (Henry Blacklock & Co., 1888).

3 Harland, *A Volume of Court Leet Records*, p. x.

4 Baines, *History of the County*, p. 105.

5 Swindells, *Manchester Streets*, vol. 4, pp. 72–3.

6 *Manchester Faces and Places* (Manchester, 1892), p. 76.

7 Ainsworth, R., *History of Ye Old Bull's Head Hotel*, Old Market Place (1923), p. 10.; Swindells, *Manchester Streets*, vol. 5, p. 86.

8 *Manchester Courier*, 6 December 1845.

9 Everett, *Panorama of Manchester*, p. 20.

10 Bowd, S., 'In the Labyrinth: John Dee and Reformation Manchester', *Manchester Region History Review*, vol. 19 (2008), p. 25.

11 Parkinson-Bailey, J., *Manchester: An Architectural History* (Manchester University Press, 2000), ch. 1; Axon, *The Annals of Manchester*, p. vi.

12 Axon, *The Annals of Manchester*, p. 39.

13 Aikin, *A Description*, p. 150.

14 Everett,, *Panorama of Manchester*, p. 129.

15 Parkinson-Bailey, *Manchester*, ch. 1.

16 Frangopulo, N., *Rich Inheritance: a guide to the history of Manchester* (Manchester Education Committee, 1962), p. 26.

17 Baines, E., *History of the Cotton Manufacture in Great Britain* (Fisher, H., Fisher, R. & Jackson, P.), 1835, p. 89.

18 Willan, T., *Elizabethan Manchester* (Manchester University Press, 1980), p. 63.

19 Mortimer, *Mercantile Manchester*, p. 2.

20 Wadsworth, A., Mann, J., *The Cotton Trade and Industrial Lancashire, 1600–1780* (Manchester University Press, 1965), ch. 1.

21 Parkinson-Bailey, *Manchester*, ch.1.

22 Swindells, *Manchester Streets*, vol 4, p. 6.

23 Harland, *A Volume of Court Leet Records*, p. x.

24 Swindells, *Manchester Streets*, vol. 4, p. 8.

25 Everett, *Panorama of Manchester*, p. 29

26 Mortimer, *Mercantile Manchester*, p. 2.

27 Bowd, *In the Labyrinth*, p. 24.

28 Axon, *The Annals of Manchester*, p. 59.

29 Parkinson-Bailey, *Manchester*, ch. 1.

30 Axon, *The Annals of Manchester,* p. 56.

31 Axon, *The Annals of Manchester*, p. 72; Baker, T., *Memorials of a Dissenting Chapel* (Simpkin, Marshall & Co., 1884).

32 Swindells, *Manchester Streets*, vol. 1, p. 104.

33 Aston, J., *A Picture of Manchester* (W.P. Aston, 1816), p. 20 & p. 86.

34 Swindells, *Manchester Streets*, vol. 1, p. 103.

35 Everett, *Panorama of Manchester*, p. 88

36 Kondo, K., 'Lost in translation? Documents relating to the disturbances at Manchester, 1715', *Manchester Region History Review*, vol. 19 (2008), p. 81.

37 Harland, J., *Collectanea Relating to Manchester and its Neighbourhood*, vol. 1 (Chetham Society, 1866).

38 Axon, *The Annals of Manchester*, p. vii. & p. 76.

39 *Manchester Times*, 4 September 1880.

40 Prentice, A., *Historical Sketches & Personal Recollections of Manchester 1792–1832* (Cass, 1970), p. 8.

INDUSTRIAL PROGRESS

From hence we came on to Manchester, one of the greatest, if not really the greatest meer village in England. It is neither a wall'd town, city, or corporation; they send no members to Parliament, and the highest magistrate they have is a constable or headborough ...

Daniel Defoe (1727)

Introduction

By around the middle of the eighteenth century Manchester was an emerging modern town with an economy increasingly dominated by textiles, and a thriving commercial focal point for the region. Traders from the surrounding towns, such as Oldham, Rochdale, Bury and Bolton, were using Manchester as the place to meet, trade and purchase goods, and most were connected to textiles in some form or another, whether it be the production of thread, unfinished cloth, engineering or chemicals. The seeds for this had already been sown, and now those seeds would bear fruit as Manchester entered an intense phase of industrial progress, often coined the Industrial Revolution. However, as the quote above by trader and writer Daniel Defoe suggests, trade was developing faster than the infrastructure to support it and this chapter looks at how Manchester adapted in order to accommodate the pressures that were being placed upon it, both in terms of urbanisation and the increased population coming to the area to work, and the drive to increase trade and commerce, which became even more prominent by the turn of the nineteenth century. Manchester's place on the global stage of world trade was causing a number of transitions including population movement from rural to urban where people were coming into the area to work and significant advances in infrastructure and technology, where new innovations forged our canals, roads and railways, as well as technology creating faster production in local factories. Economically and socially, local society was fractured by class distinction, and a person's place in the economic and social pecking order was played out in every aspect of daily life. Terms such as 'Cottonopolis' and 'Shock City' were now being used to describe Manchester. This chapter takes the story from around the 1750s to the 1830s, and this period in particular saw both industry and society revolutionise on a scale previously unseen.

Manchester Goods and Manchester Men

By the middle of the eighteenth century, commerce in the region was a thriving and increasingly organised operation, and the area was already a well-known centre for 'Manchester goods'. These goods were distributed by 'Manchester men', a network of merchants that retailed at fairs and other markets. Manchester was rapidly becoming a key centre for finishing and marketing of textiles goods produced in the surrounding towns and villages, as the historian Jon Stobart explains:

> All this implies an extensive region, with Manchester acting as a centre of control for textile production across eastern and central Lancashire. The regional space economy was thus drawn together through the flows of goods, credit and capital which centred on Manchester warehouses, dye houses and the Exchange.[1]

The structure of the textile industry, particularly up to 1800, had mainly comprised cottage-based production financed by Manchester merchants, who supplied raw cotton to spinners. This arrangement worked because it overcame the transport problems that existed in a society that was yet to develop suitable means of mobility for people and goods. Commercial travellers and merchants travelled around the region, presenting prospective buyers with samples and taking orders. They travelled on packhorses to the main towns and from shop to shop selling their goods, and often stored unsold goods at local inns.[2] However, both the condition and lack of any proper road network impeded their ability to trade more widely. The advent of turnpike roads improved the ability to get around more efficiently and horse-drawn waggons appeared, which allowed country manufacturers and merchants to travel about more easily with their pattern books and collecting orders, and from around the 1730s they were able to cover most of Britain.

From the 1770s, the cotton industry truly accelerated, and this was mainly due to technological improvements to machinery, such as the first steam-powered cotton mill built by Richard Arkwright around 1782 on Miller Street, which performed the cording and spinning of cotton. The emergence of the factory system speeded up and rationalised production and allowed more places to sell an increased range of products and trade overseas.[3] There is no doubt that the middle to the end of the eighteenth century was a time awash with inventions, and the region's innovators were busily creating machinery that would make the textiles process more productive. In 1733, John Kay, a Bury engineer, created an early invention in the form of the fly-shuttle used in weaving. This led to an imbalance where cloth could be woven quicker than the thread could be spun, and each process had to improve to keep up. In 1764, James Hargreaves, a Blackburn weaver, invented the Spinning Jenny; in 1779, Samuel Crompton of Bolton invented another spinning machine in the form of the Mule. However, new forms of production were not universally welcome and led to the damaging of machines and social disturbances as machinery was putting people out of work. The Luddites formed in response to concerns over being made unemployed and the worry of having enough money to feed their families. John Kay moved to Paris after being harassed and victimised, and Hargreaves moved to Nottingham. In 1779, workers went on a spree of destroying Spinning Jennies and any machine that could be seen to lead to unemployment.[4]

Manufacturers required open access to new markets, and during the second half of the eighteenth century there was a substantial increase in foreign trade, thereby increasing overseas travel and foreign merchants visiting both the United Kingdom and locally, securing Manchester's cosmopolitan credentials as a global leader in trade.[5] The importance of Liverpool and its port from the early eighteenth century ensured that the two towns were interlinked in the region's commercial expansion, certainly until the Manchester Ship Canal was opened late in the nineteenth century, but up until then Manchester's trade very much depended on goods going to and from Liverpool's docks. By the 1760s, overseas cotton markets were opened up, with raw cotton from the West Indies and colonies in Brazil, Mauritius and Turkey.[6] By the 1780s, cotton trade started from the East Indies and North America. Other industries that contributed to the whole textiles process rapidly developed, and innovations in bleaching became an important part of cotton finishing. Those engaged in this were known as 'whisters' and it is estimated that around fifty were attending the Manchester markets in the 1780s. Spinning was originally separated from weaving, but increasingly firms were combining these different processes under the same roof. For those that kept the manufacturing processes separate, yarn was sold to a manufacturer through a yarn agent, a middleman in commercial practices.

Commercial Organisation

Merchants and manufacturers became organised through a series of committees and trade societies to deal with key commercial issues, and these included the Manchester Committee for the Protection and Encouragement of Trade formed in 1774. In 1772, the Detection and Prosecution of Felons and Receivers of Stolen and Embezzled Goods was established to keep workers in check should they be tempted to engage in deception against their employers. Protecting trade interests at global level was increasingly important for merchants, and from the latter part of the eighteenth century a rash of commercial organisations emerged to ensure the protection of trade interests. The Manchester Commercial Society of 1794 met the first Thursday of each month at Spencer's Tavern to discuss protection of their interests in overseas trade. The Manchester Chamber of Commerce was established in 1820 and has stood the test of time as it is still in existence today.[7]

The main market day was Tuesday when all the merchants from around the region would descend on Manchester, and this led to informal gatherings of merchants from all over the region, who stayed at Manchester's inns and public houses. Thomas Swindells, in his memoirs of Manchester life, gives an insight into the role of the public house in commercial activity on market days. He describes the role of 'hookers-in', who were pressure salesmen who would seek out new arrivals at inns and public houses and encourage country manufacturers to visit the numerous warehouses that they were representing. It seems clear that there was much to be made with a proactive sales approach, as he describes how:

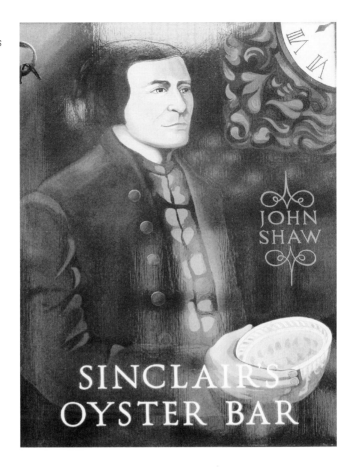

The merchants in those days adopted another means of securing the attendance of buyers at their warehouses. As soon as it was known that a probable customer had arrived in town, which could be ascertained by a reference to the way-bills of the coaches recently arrived, a clerk was dispatched to interview the visitor. It is on record that one gentleman who had arrived overnight from London was honoured one morning before breakfast by no fewer than forty such callers. Needless to say the custom rapidly developed into a nuisance, and many were the indignant protests made by victims of it.[8]

Inns provided a range of services for travelling merchants and some even initiated formalised clubs. One of the most famous of these was John Shaw's club. John Shaw was a publican of the eighteenth century who had a tavern in the Shambles, which became known as John Shaw's Punch House. Shaw's tavern became a popular meeting place for merchants eager to exchange news and views, and his famous punch drink was a particular attraction. Shaw was not only a publican, but one who had awareness of civic responsibility and was elected to a local office.[9] Despite Shaw's death in 1796, not long after the club's initiation, the tradition was continued, moving from inn to inn as circumstances changed, until 1938 when, after over 200 years, the club finally disbanded. Shaw and his family were buried at St Ann's church and a plaque on the outer wall commemorates his role in Manchester life. He is also featured on the inn sign of Sinclair's Oyster Bar in the current Exchange Square (figure 25), along with his housekeeper, Molly Maid, who was known to harass customers with her mop should they attempt to stay after closing. The Scramble Club was another informal social means of merchants meeting. What began as regular lunch at Old Froggatt's at the Unicorn on Church Street, became a dining club from around 1806, for younger merchants and tradesmen who were relative newcomers to business. They attended around 1 p.m. in the afternoon and enjoyed 4-penny pies and ale. Eventually they all made contributions to pay for a proper joint of meat. By Christmas 1810, they had formed a more formalised club which was coined the Scramble Club owing to the rush to business after their lunchtime meal.

The Manchester Exchange

The Manchester (Royal) Exchange is one of the most impressive buildings in central Manchester and today houses the Royal Exchange Theatre Company. Originally, it was foremost a trading centre that lasted until 1968. The first Manchester Exchange was built in 1729 by the Lord of the Manor, Sir Oswald Mosley, and was located close to the end of Market Street. We do not know a great deal about the structure of the original building, other than sketches of the outside, but over the course of the eighteenth century it was gradually deserted, and was pulled down in 1792. Despite this, the site was still a popular place for merchants and country manufacturers to meet, and Tuesday at noon remained the key trading time of the week. This first Exchange catered for a range of trades, including cotton production, printing, shipping and so on. There were problems with the first attempt at a commercial institution in Manchester, since despite its impressive façade, the first Exchange could not be utilised effectively owing to small, overcrowded and unpleasant streets that surrounded it, which became even more clogged with market stallholders.[10]

26 Market Place with the original Manchester Exchange on the right. (Courtesy of Manchester Libraries, Information and Archives, Manchester City Council)

The end of the first Exchange from 1790 resulted in the absence of any formalised commercial institution of this kind until its replacement in 1809. In the interim, merchants congregated at a site that became known as 'Penniless Hill', close to the original Exchange site. Subsequently, a room was provided near St Ann's Square in which to conduct business, but the development of trade soon made these meagre facilities insufficient. Plans for a new Exchange soon followed and a meeting to discuss the development of a new Exchange building and to raise funds took place at Spencer's Tavern on 8 October 1804; from here subscriptions were raised to pay for the new building, which opened on 1 January 1809. The development of the Manchester Exchange post-1809 was rapid, with several modifications to its design to meet the ever-growing demands placed upon it. There appeared to be little long-term consideration to the usage of the building, with one expansion no sooner completed than other plans were initiated, and the impression was of Manchester's commercial activity being forever invincible, becoming an iconic symbol of Manchester's place in world trade.

Close by was the Corn and Produce Exchange. Originally built in 1837, it was the centre for trading in food stuffs. Before 1837, food was sold in the markets around Hanging Ditch but this building improved the facilities around this area and brought much of the trade indoors. The original building was demolished and rebuilt between 1897 and 1903. Today it is a Grade II listed building which houses the fashionable Triangle shopping and restaurant centre.

So far, the story is one of rapid progress in trade and commerce, but the infrastructure of the town was impeding further progress. Specifically, the poor transport network was holding the region back, so that improvements were essential in order to cope with the demands of both trade and people. A range of different transport services emerged over the course of the century from the 1750s, such as road transport in the form of coaching services, but these were

27 Manchester Exchange, St Ann's Square.

28 The former Corn Exchange.

limited in both their services and journey times. Workers in villages had been traditionally employed locally so there had been little need for a formalised transport system, and even during the early days of factory working many still walked to work since their jobs were within their immediate community, in part because their long hours of work and low pay restricted their employment options.[11] Therefore, working-class people had little need to travel, apart from the occasional trip to a market, but even then it was often within walking distance. Transport that was available serviced a middle- and upper-class clientele, particularly those engaged in commerce who travelled more widely and moved between villages, towns and cities in order to develop their businesses. Not only was the need to travel not so great for the majority, the high cost of stage coach travel in the nineteenth century deterred ordinary working folk from using this form of transport. For example, in the early nineteenth century a two-horse coach from St Ann's Square to Cheetham Hill was 5 shillings and the cost of toll bars 8 pence. Usually a further sixpence was needed as a tip for the driver, so a journey could be expensive, and consequently restricted the number of services that were available, particularly within urban areas that were easily accessed by foot.[12]

However, progress was made and by the turn of the nineteenth century a well-established network of both regional and national towns and cities had linked up with Manchester through a number of coaching inns. Large coaching inns tended to offer journeys over long distances, such as to London, and the smaller inns and pubs catered for more localised routes. Coaches were run by innkeepers all over the country who operated in partnership with each other.[13] Most of the larger hostelries offering transport services were located on the main streets in the heart of the commercial district, between Piccadilly, along Market Street towards the Manchester Exchange. The large coaching inns that serviced destinations further afield included the Bridgewater Arms on High Street, the Mosley Arms, Palace Inn, the Swan Inn, Flying Horse and Talbot Inn, all located in Market Street, the Old Boar's Head in Hyde's Cross, the Star Inn on Deansgate and the White Bear in Piccadilly.[14] Smaller inns and pubs offered more localised journeys on the main arterial routes out of central Manchester, such as Deansgate, Withy Grove and Shudehill, to other major towns in the area, such as Oldham, Rochdale, Stockport, Bolton and beyond. For example, the Hare and Hounds on Shudehill covered routes through Oldham to Saddleworth.[15] Equally, the Lower Turk's Head in Shudehill and the Three Crowns in Cockgates also offered a number of services to Oldham, Middleton, Rochdale and Bury. Of the major coaching inns, the Bridgewater Arms was the foremost hostelry and Manchester's leading transport centre for over fifty years. During the late eighteenth century several major services ran from here, and during the nineteenth century it serviced journeys all over the country, including Birmingham, Glasgow, and London.[16] Services also included the London Royal Mail Coach, which stopped at various points en route. The Carlisle mail coaching service called at Lancaster, and other services included the Liverpool and York Royal Mail services. By the 1820s, the Bridgewater Arms had become one of the most notable transport centres in the area, offering postal and carriage services, and could accommodate around 100 people requiring an overnight stay. The landlord of the Bridgewater Arms at this time was Henry Charles Lacey. He proved to be a successful businessman in transport services and an advertisement in *Pigot and Dean's* 1821 trade directory shows him promoting a range of services from both the Bridgewater Arms and the nearby Palace Inn, where he offered all manner of postal services and different types of vehicles including barouches, landaus, and even hearses and mourning coach services. Other major coaching inns included the Mosley Arms on Market Street, and here destinations on offer included Sheffield,

Leeds, Nottingham and Lancaster. The Palace, Talbot and Star Inns also operated similar destinations and services.[17] Further along Market Street was the Swan Inn and coach office, which at its peak had over five services to London daily and from which well-known coaches such as the *Peveril of the Peak* and the *Red Rover* ran. Local commentator, Edwin Waugh, described the Star Inn in his memoirs as one of the oldest and largest hotels in Manchester, which during the coaching days did the second largest amount of business after the Royal and Bridgewater Arms. It was a place of high status, where local gentry met and socialised, and was also close to a noted barracks and military headquarters. In particular, it was a place where notable men in the legal profession stayed.[18]

Coaches were distinctive and usually painted red and black, with each being drawn by four horses. Their guards and coachmen were well presented, dressed in red coats and hats, decorated with broad gilt hat bands and top boots. Coach names were very much part of the culture of transport services with names like the *Eclipse*, *Red Rover*, *Royal Sovereign*, *Champion*, *Perseverance* and *Highflyer* to name just a few. The *Peveril of the Peak* was a popular coach that was a particularly attractive sight riding through Manchester because of the four fine piebald horses that drove it. Josiah Slugg, who lived in Market Street in the first half of the nineteenth century and recorded his reminiscences, commented on the fact that he knew the time simply because of the arrival or departure of the coaches such was their good timekeeping and reliability.[19] By the 1830s, improvements to coaches meant that journey times had been cut dramatically and by this time coaches to London arrived the same day.[20] Considering that in 1760 a journey to London would have taken three days, two days by 1779 and 30 hours by 1799, by 1836 it was taking a mere 18 hours, so there had been considerable progress in reducing journey times by road.[21] Descriptive insights into the typical daily hustle and bustle of coaching inns are seen in the novel *The Manchester Man* by Isabella Linnaeus Banks. It vividly describes a journey starting from the Palace Inn at the top of Market Street, and is a scene that was repeated several times each day:

> The open space in front was enlivened by the newly painted London stage-coach, the 'Lord Nelson', the fresh scarlet coats of coachmen and guards, the assembling of passengers and luggage, the shouting and swearing of half-awake oastlers and porters, the grumbling of the first-corners (shivering in the raw air) at the unpunctuality of the state, the excuses of the booking-clerk, the self-gratulations of the last arrival that he was 'in time', the dragging of trunks and portmanteaus on to the top,

the thrusting of bags and boxes into the boot, the harnessing of snorting steeds the horsing of the vehicle, the scrambling of the 'outsiders' to the top by the ladder and wheel, the self-satisfied settlement of the 'insides' in the places they had 'booked for', the crushing and thrusting of friends with last messages and parting words, the crack of the whip, the sound of the bugle, the prancing of horses, the rattle of wheels, and dashing off up Market Street Lane of the gallant four-in-hand, amid the hurrahs of excited spectators. Every morning witnessed a somewhat similar scene of bustle and excitement at five o'clock when the London coach started.[22]

Another important development in local transport was that of the canals, which became instrumental in the carriage of goods, particularly heavy cargo such as coal. The Bridgewater Canal was constructed around 1758 after an Act of Parliament was passed that allowed a canal to be built between Worsley and Salford, and a deviation from Worsley to Manchester via Stretford. It was originally intended for carrying coal, and James Brindley was given the task of undertaking the civil engineering project. He faced a number of engineering challenges but the result was a canal that cut the costs of coal in half because of much reduced transport costs. Even before the original canal was completed an additional branch was begun by extending the canal from Stretford to the River Mersey at Runcorn. Other canals in the region were constructed, including the Manchester, Bolton and Bury Canal that began life in the 1790s; the Manchester, Ashton and Oldham Canal that began in 1792; and the Rochdale Canal in 1794.

On 15 September 1830, a transport revolution began when the first railway between Manchester and Liverpool opened. It was a momentous achievement and heralded a whole new way of life for the passage of goods and people. The terminus in Manchester was on Liverpool Road, which became a large railway station and is currently the site of the Museum of Science and Industry, where one can step back in time and stand in the original station ticket hall. It was unfortunate that the first day of the railways also led to the first fatality when the Rt-Hon. William Huskisson, who was on the first train, died of his injuries when, during a refreshment stop between Manchester and Liverpool, he was distracted and did not see an oncoming train. Despite this fatality and unfortunate start, it did not prevent the network from developing. Liverpool Road Station opened in 1830, followed by Hunt's Bank (later Victoria) and Store Street (later London Road/Piccadilly) stations in the early 1840s. Victoria Station opened on 1 January 1844 and was made larger in 1864.

29 Former Liverpool Road Station, currently the Museum of Science and Industry.

30 The opening of the Manchester and Liverpool railway, 1830. (Courtesy of Manchester Libraries, Information and Archives, Manchester City Council)

31 Victoria Station, Hunt's Bank.

Early journeys on the railways, particularly with an incomplete network, could be fraught with difficulties and this is what John Bull Junior shared with readers of the *Manchester Courier* in 1838, in which his article on 'railway groans' gives insight that all was not straightforward developing such an important innovation. Overcrowding was a problem, as was confusion over luggage at stations.[23] The amount of land required for railway development also created problems. The Earl of Derby was one of the largest landowners in Lancashire and a number of railway companies had to negotiate land purchases so that lines and stations could be constructed.[24]

Urban Development

From the 1750s, Manchester was rapidly increasing both in terms of geographical spread and its population. Figure 32 (page 84) is a map of the centre during the latter part of the eighteenth century which illustrates the scale of Manchester and its immediate vicinity. In terms of population, the town was increasing on a significant scale, and by the 1750s the estimated population was around 20,000 rising to 50,000 by the end of the 1700s.[25] By the first official census in 1801, this had risen again to around 95,000.[26] By the 1790s, Manchester had been divided into a series of districts, and these are illustrated in Table 1.

District No.	District Name	Description of Location
1	New Cross	Ancoats Lane, Newton Lane
2	St Michael's	Newton Lane, Swan St, Miller's Lane, Long Millgate
3	Collegiate Church	Long Millgate, Hanging Ditch, Cateaton Street
4	St Clement's	Piccadilly, Lever Street, Ancoats Lane
5	St Paul's	Lever Street, New Cross, Swan Street, Shudehill, Nicholas Croft, High Street
6	Exchange	St Mary's Gate, Deansgate, Cateaton Street, Withy Grove, Nicholas Croft, High Street
7	Minshull	Piccadilly, Bank Top, Garrett Lane, Brook St
8	St James	Levers Row, Garrett Lane, Bond Street, Fountain Street
9	St Ann's	St Mary's Gate, Market Street, Fountain Street, Brasennose Street, Princess Street, Deansgate
10	Oxford St	Bond Street, Brook Street, Dawson Street
11	St Peter's	Dawson Street, Alport Street, Deansgate
12	St Mary's	Salford Bridge, Deansgate, Bridge Street
13	Old Quay	Bridge Street, Deansgate, Quay Street
14	St John's	Quay Street, Alport Street, Rivers Irwell & Medlock

Table 1: District boundaries based on the 'Commissioners under the Police Act' meeting held at the Bull's Head, 18 July 1792. (Source: *MCRL, M117/181A Register of Beer etc Retailers A, B, C & D divisions 1869 C16.2.*)

Market Street, the area around Collegiate Church, and the Exchange district were developing a more commercial focus consisting of shopkeepers and tradesmen, and the development of the Manchester Exchange in St Ann's Square increased its reputation as a commercial district. St Paul's parish district was located between Piccadilly and New Cross, bordering Oldham Street. This district was noted for its concentration of warehouses, reinforcing it as a significant trading area. St James's parish was located at the other side of Piccadilly and contained Mosley Street, which was noted for larger dwellings and some of Manchester's

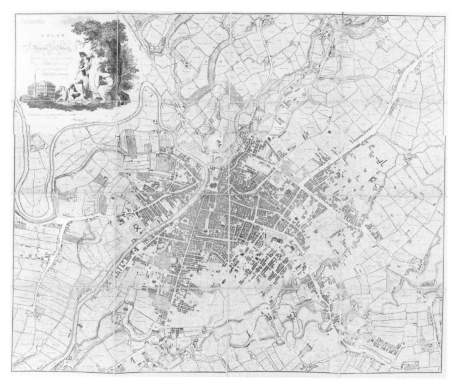

32 Map of Manchester, *c.* 1787. (Copyright University of Manchester)

finer buildings, where a number of Manchester's merchant class resided in the
early part of the century, but as they migrated out to the suburbs many of their fine
dwellings became warehouses. St Michael's parish district was close to Rochdale
Road (or St George's Road, as it was formerly known), north of the centre, bordering the township of Cheetham.[27] Here, housing was generally back-to-back, with
narrow unpaved streets, and inhabited by the poor, and was associated with low
types of hostelries, particularly beerhouses which had become a feature of drinking culture after the 1830 Beer Act which allowed hundreds of beerhouse to open
that just sold beer and were often places of ill repute. According to the *Manchester
Guardian*, St Michael's Ward was inhabited 'principally by the operative class, a
great portion by thieves, beggars and prostitutes'.[28] St Clement's district bordered
Ancoats, and contained many mills and workshops, along with pubs and beerhouses, with similar characteristics to St Michael's. Shudehill had become a key
market and wholesale area for food stuffs. In 1775, an Act of Parliament was
passed to widen and develop some of Manchester's main streets and in 1821 further improvements were made to Market Street.[29]

These parishes were also accompanied by a series of outer districts that had once been hamlets or small villages but had been consumed by Manchester's urban development. Places such as Ancoats, which was located just north-east of the city centre, had once been a rural hamlet but by the early nineteenth century was an extensive factory district predominantly engaged in textile manufacturing, and contained many of the large cotton mills, such as McConnel and Kennedy, and Murrays. It is therefore no surprise to see a great deal of working-class housing springing up around the mills. Housing was often thrown up, and mainly consisted of back-to-back dwellings.[30] Great Ancoats Street was the main highway through the district, which linked New Cross at the bottom of Oldham Road and Ardwick. Ardwick, like Ancoats, contained a number of mills and areas of working-class housing. It had also once been an affluent area in a rural setting, but was increasingly subsumed by Manchester's urban development and overtaken by heavy industries such as ironworks, brickworks and chemical plants. Ardwick was effectively cut in two with the building of railways, creating Higher and Lower Ardwick. Newton Heath was a working-class district that bordered Oldham Road and was known for its low-cost back-to-back housing and industry. Its close proximity to the Rochdale Canal resulted in the development of industries such as glass, soap and engineering. Again, the development of railways changed the landscape where two main lines cut through the area, and consequently Newton Heath became noted for engineering and the skilled labour associated with the railway industry. Cheetham was north of the centre of Manchester and was a relatively desirable place to live at the time, becoming associated with wealthy industrialists building their homes there.

Manchester society had begun to split between mill workers and mill owners, a working class and a middle class. Mosley Street in the eighteenth century was the residential location of Manchester's richest and had been architecturally laid out from around 1750. However, in the first quarter of the nineteenth century it began to lose its residential status as the middle class began to move out to the affluent suburbs that were emerging, such as South Manchester and Pendleton, facilitated by a better transport system that allowed the richer inhabitant to commute. Businesses and warehouses took over the large vacated houses and this led to a shift in aspects of Manchester's commerce, since the business district around High Street and Market Street was by now migrating to the Mosley Street area. The intellectual and cultural life of the town flowered from the seeds of newfound wealth created by a middle class that had the money to spend and a lifestyle to enjoy. They were not only commercially talented but culturally and intellectually aware, and often politically minded, as class and political debates became significant issues for a society beginning to divide on the basis of a person's occupation and financial status.

This affluence, however, did not apply to everyone, and conditions for working-class people who were increasingly living in poor housing and working in the new and unregulated factories were very different. Increased population, overcrowding, and insanitary conditions inevitably resulted in outbreaks of disease and this became such as problem that measures were quickly needed to regain control of local public health. In 1752, subscriptions began for the building of an infirmary. A house was purchased close to Shudehill and Withy Grove which opened as a hospital on 24 June 1752. In 1754, land in Piccadilly was purchased from Oswald Mosley in order for a larger purpose-built hospital to be constructed. This opened in 1755, and facilities were added to it over subsequent decades. This new infirmary could accommodate around eighty patients and by 1834 it had been enlarged to accommodate 160 patients. Adjoining the infirmary was the lunatic hospital and asylum, and the Manchester dispensary. In 1796, a movement began to establish Manchester's fever hospital, and several cottages in Portland Street were purchased to receive fever victims. This proved so successful that subscriptions were raised to build a proper hospital in Aytoun Street, which opened in 1804. It closed around 1856 as other hospitals replaced its services.[31] There were other dispensaries created in the locality, including the Chorlton-upon-Medlock dispensary established in 1827, and the Ardwick and Ancoats Dispensary established in 1828, and the

33 New Bailey Prison. (Courtesy of Manchester Libraries, Information and Archives, Manchester City Council)

Hulme Dispensary.[32] Many towns had workhouses, the place where the unemployed poor went when they were totally destitute. As a rapidly growing place, Manchester was faced with the problem of what to do with the destitute. There is evidence of a pauper workhouse in 1754 in Manchester.[33] However, the main workhouse was constructed following the 1790 Manchester Poor House Act, and was built on New Bridge Street and opened in 1793.[34] The previous chapter referred to the former New Fleet Prison at Hunt's Bank, which closed in 1774, and a new prison in the form of the New Bailey was opened. On 22 May 1787, the foundation stone was laid by Thomas Butterworth Bayley, and the first intake of prisoners was in 1790.[35] The infamous New Bailey Prison was located on the border with Salford and became a notorious place for inmates. Prisoners were employed in some tasks, but it was an unpleasant experience, and where they were faced with the treadmill, a device in which fifteen prisoners operated eight wheels to rasp dye-woods. The water supply needed to drive this was stored at the top of the building and it was little short of torture to operate. By 1816, the prison was deemed insufficient and was enlarged, with the outside being made more secure for fear of a breakout.[36]

Conclusion

Manchester during the eighteenth and early nineteenth centuries became a vibrant place where the industrial process was in full swing and rapid urbanisation and population increases were shaping the geography of the locality. The infrastructure of the town was developing to keep pace with industrial progress, but only just. However, local life was not just about trade and commerce. Society had begun to divide, based on the haves and have nots, where middle- and working-class people were living very different lives in the same locality. This created a range of social and political issues that were about to spill over into mass confrontation with the authorities, and it is here that the story moves, to consider the implications of industrial progress.

Notes

1 Stobart, J., 'Manchester and its region: networks and boundaries in the eighteenth century', *Manchester Region History Review*, vol. 19 (2008), pp. 66–80.

2 Aikin, *A Description*, p. 183.

3 Swindells, *Manchester Streets*, vol. 4, p. 97.

4 Faucher, L., *Manchester in 1844: its present condition and future prospects* (Cass, 1844), pp. 5–6.

5 Aikin, *A Description*, p. 184.

6 Mortimer, *Mercantile Manchester*, pp. 5–6.

7 Redford, *Manchester Merchants*, p. 2, 17.

8 Swindells, *Manchester Streets*, vol. 3, p. 105.

9 Stancliffe, F.S., *John Shaw's* (Sherratt & Hughes, 1938), p. 18–21.

10 Scott, R., *The Biggest Room in the World: a short history of the Manchester Royal Exchange* (Royal Exchange Theatre Trust, 1976), p. 9.

11 Manchester Corporation Transport Department, *A Hundred Years of Road Passenger Transport in Manchester* (1935), p. 7.

12 Manchester Corporation, *A Hundred Years*, p. 3.

13 Barker, T.C., Gerhold, D., *The Rise and Rise of Road Transport, 1700–1990* (Cambridge University Press, 1993), p. 58; Barker, T.C. and Savage, C.I., *An Economic History of Transport in Britain* (Routledge, 1974); Chartres, J. & Turnbull, G., 'Road Transport', in Aldcroft, D. and M. Freeman (eds), *Transport in Victorian Britain* (Manchester University Press, 1983); Bagwell, P.S., *The Transport Revolution from 1770* (Batsford, 1974).

14 Love, B., *Manchester as it is* (Love and Barton, 1839), p. 239.; Swindells, *Manchester Streets*, vol.1, pp. 196–7.

15 Baines, E., *History, Directory and Gazetteer of the Palatine County of Lancashire* (W. Wales, 1825), pp. 397–412.

16 Baines, *History, Directory and Gazetteer*, pp. 397–412.

17 *Pigot & Dean Trade Directory 1821/2*; Baines, E., *History, Directory, & Gazetteer of the County Palatine of Lancaster* (Liverpool, 1825); Swindells, *Manchester Streets*, vol. 2, pp. 98–9.

18 Hayes, L., *Reminiscences of Manchester from the year 1840* (Sherratt & Hughes, 1905), p. 131; *Manchester Times*, 18 December 1880.

19 Slugg, J., *Reminiscences of Manchester Fifty years Ago* (Cornish, 1881), pp. 10, 212–13.

20 *Manchester & Salford Advertiser*, 23 November 1833.

21 Aston, J., *The Manchester Guide: A Brief Historical Description of the Towns of Manchester & Salford, the Public Buildings, and the Charitable and Literary Institutions* (Joseph Aston, 1804), p. 93; *Manchester Mercury and Harrop's General Advertiser,* 16 November 1779; *Manchester Mercury*, 18 June 1799; Dyos, H. & Aldcroft, D., *British Transport: an economic survey from the seventeenth century to the twentieth* (Penguin Books, 1969), p. 75.

22 Linnaeus Banks, G., *The Manchester Man* (E.J. Morten publishers, 1896).

23 *Manchester Courier*, 1 September 1838.

24 Kellet, *The Impact of Railways*, p. 151–2.

25 Everett, *Panorama of Manchester*, p. 41–2

26 Data taken from (1831) The Complete Account of the Population of Great Britain (348), and (1901) Census of England and Wale [Cd.616], *House of Commons Parliamentary Papers.*

27 Love, *Manchester*, p. 53.

28 *Manchester Guardian*, 26 July 1854.

29 Baines, *History, Directory, & Gazetteer*, p. 130.

30 Kidd, A., *Manchester* (Edinburgh University Press, 2002), p. 16.

31 Swindells, *Manchester Streets*, vol 2, pp. 13, 79.

32 Everett, *Panorama of Manchester*, p. 104.

33 Hindle, G.B., *Provision for the Relief of the Poor in Manchester, 1754-1826* (Chetham's Society, 1975), p. 1.

34 See workhouses.org.uk/Manchester/; Hindle, *Provision for the Relief*, p. 1.

35 Swindells, *Manchester Streets*, p. 117.

36 Everett, *Panorama of Manchester*, p. 212.

POLITICS AND PROTEST

In ten minutes from the commencement of the havoc the field was an open and almost deserted space. The sun looked down through a sultry and motionless air. The curtains and blinds of the windows within view were all closed. The hustings remained, with a few broken and hewed flag-staves erect, and a torn and gashed banner or two dropping; whilst over the whole field were strewed caps, bonnets, hats, shawls, and shoes, and other parts of male and female dress, trampled, torn, and bloody. Several mounds of human being still remained where they had fallen, crushed down and smothered. Some of these still groaning, others with staring eyes, were gasping for breath, and others would never breathe more. All was silent save those low sounds, and the occasional snorting and pawing of steeds.

Samuel Bamford (1864)

Introduction

The opening quote is a description of the scene at St Peter's Field by the Middleton radical Samuel Bamford, whose testimony provides one perspective of events at the Peterloo Massacre on 16 August 1819. This meeting, which resulted in around eleven dead and several hundred injured, was the culmination of popular discontent that had been simmering from the late eighteen century. The scene it conveys is one of chaos and distress and it show how Manchester was a politically volatile place in the early part of the nineteenth century. This is hardly surprising, given the march of industrialism on a workforce that was first-hand witnesses to changes in work practices, conditions and deprivation. Lack of a political voice to improve the situation of the working class exacerbated a groundswell of discontent amongst a group who increasingly felt aggrieved that they were toiling to create wealth but felt none of the advantages of their efforts, and this spilled out in political restlessness and clashes with the authorities. However, the politics of the time was not just about working-class discontent. The middle class were also vocal in expressing political concerns and campaigned vigorously when they felt due cause. They were also dissatisfied with the limitations of the voting system, and felt that Manchester, as a city of newfound wealth creators, should be politically represented in Parliament. The middle class were also ardent supporters of free trade; and when there were problems with the Corn Laws, none other than Richard Cobden established the Anti-Corn Law League to protest against the suffering the Corn Laws were causing working-class people who were struggling to afford a loaf of bread. This chapter looks at the phase from the turn of the nineteenth century to the 1840s, in which we lead up to and see the aftermath of the Peterloo Massacre, the effects of the Great Reform Act of 1832 and how this affected Manchester's representation in Parliament, through to the onset of Chartism in the region, and middle-class political campaigns.

Early Radical Politics

Thomas Swindells, in his five-volume work on *Manchester Streets and Manchester Men,* stated:

> The population of the town a century ago was divided into two classes, the somebodies and the nobodies. The line of demarcation was most rigidly drawn and the wives and daughters of the wealthy avoided contact with the majority of the population, except on such special occasions when they condescended to patronise them.[1]

He was not the first to makes such an observation and during the nineteenth century Manchester had attracted a number of well-educated observers whose amazement and horror came in equal measure. They were so in awe yet horrified at this new industrial and urban society that they toured the area to record their findings. One such visitor was the French political thinker and writer, Alexis de Tocqueville, who commented that:

> The greatest stream of human industry flows out to fertilise the whole world. From this filthy sewer pure gold flows. Here humanity attains its most complete development and its most brutish; here civilisation works its miracles, and civilised man is turned back into a savage.[2]

The factory system was indeed a cruel existence: long hours, a very unhealthy environment at best, often extremely dangerous with limbs regularly damaged or lost. Both women and men were employed in cotton mills, and even young children were useful in getting inside the smallest of spaces in and underneath the machinery. Often pregnant women were at the point of giving birth and still working, then back in the factory within hours of bringing their child into the world. Families relied on grandparents and other family members to look after children whilst their parents worked, and laudanum, or Godfrey's syrup as it was commonly referred to (and a form of opium), was administered to keep babies quiet.

But was this always the case? Well, whilst not disputing that life for some was pretty awful, working-class people certainly worked hard and they also played hard after an arduous working day, which often led them to a local pub or beer-house. Concerns over this type of behaviour led to middle-class attempts at social improvement. Some have argued that the middle class were genuinely concerned about working-class welfare, since a healthy and happy workforce is a productive one, yet others focus on a patronising attempt at forcing a moral Victorian respectability onto a class whose standards needed raising to middle-class virtues, which were so prevalent in Victorian society. Journalist and writer William Cooke-Taylor, who toured Lancashire in 1841, described how 'it (Manchester) is essentially a place of business, where pleasure is unknown as a pursuit and amusements scarcely rank as secondary consideration'.[3] The pub provided sociability but it also provided an opportunity for working-class people to air their discontent amongst themselves.

The French Revolution in 1789 had created a profound effect in England. It gave the ordinary poor working person hope that they could also achieve greater economic and political democracy in this country too. Therefore, it is no surprise that when political activist Thomas Paine's *Rights of Man* was published in 1791, just two years after the events in France, it became so popular and widely read in Manchester, and was discussed at a range of newly emerging societies. Groups wanting radical political change in society often rubbed shoulders with those who were resistant to any change, and as we saw earlier, these 'Church and King' men met regularly at the Bull's Head Inn. The industrial process rapidly affected the lives of ordinary workers, the mechanisation of spinning and weaving had negatively impacted on the employment of many, and their grievances were often played out in the emergence of unions, protests for political rights and even food riots. An example of this was in the summer of 1795, when at a time of high bread prices and food shortages riots broke out in Market Place and New Cross and the cavalry were called in to intervene, resulting in a number of injuries. The cavalry at this time were a severe bunch of often ill-trained volunteers who suppressed discontent quite violently, as was witnessed in Bamford's vivid account of Peterloo.[4] The Manchester Exchange was mobbed in April 1812 when a meeting to celebrate the Prince Regent's retention of the Tory government was hastily cancelled through fear of a disturbance, but unfortunately they were too late and the Exchange was invaded and vandalised, resulting in the military being called in to restore order. This riot was very symbolic in where it took place, hitting the heart of the business community. This incident occurred around the time that the machine-breaking Luddites were active in Lancashire, creating an air of unrest.

There were key phases in Manchester's radical political life. The first was that leading up to and culminating in the Peterloo Massacre. The 1820s was a quieter but nonetheless active phase where tactics switched from physical action to one of abstinence from taxable products to hit the government financially. During the 1830s there were some concessions from the government, ultimately leading to the Great Reform Act of 1832 where the right to vote was extended to some groups, most notably the middle class, and Manchester finally gained a voice in Parliament by having two MPs represent the area, in Mark Philips and Charles Poulett Thomson. However, the legislation was insufficient and did not go far enough, leading to the development of Chartism, a group who, as their name implies, set up a charter containing six key points: vote by secret ballot; no property qualification; payment of MPs; constituencies of equal size; annual parliaments; the right to vote for every man over 21. Chartism was clearly felt in Manchester as a mechanism for going forward in the desire for democracy. So here we see Chartism flourish into the 1830s and 1840s.

The right to vote had depended on your wealth, in particular the land you owned and your upper-class credentials. The new urban context had arrived much quicker than slow-moving institutions such as Parliament could keep pace with, and it left towns such as Manchester emerging with not only a working class, but a middle class who equally wanted a greater political say, since after all they, not the aristocracy, were now the wealth creators of the nation. By 1815, the Napoleonic Wars had ended after over two decades of conflict. Soldiers returning from the battlefield came back to unemployment, hardship and poverty, entrenching even further deep-rooted discontent. In 1817, the Blanketeers, a group of textile workers petitioning the Prince Regent about the state of their industry, marched to London, and a large gathering in March of the same year was convened on St Peter's Field in support of their protest. However, the authorities, fearing revolution, dispersed the crowd.

Workplace discipline severely restricted communication as much as did the overwhelming noise and a poor working environment, so working-class people had no option but to find alternative places to meet and discuss issues of common interest. Political gatherings became common if somewhat undercover, and public houses became a convenient and often the only location for working-class radicals to meet, particularly during the earlier phase of radical political activity. Some of these early radical meetings in public houses were described by Manchester commentator and newspaper proprietor Archibald Prentice, who recalled a meeting that was arranged in May 1812 by the leading local radical John Knight at the Elephant public house in Tib Street, the aim of which was to discuss radical demands, such as parliamentary reform and the relief of working-class distress. This meeting was both formal and well organised, with the appointment of a committee whose ultimate intention was to petition Parliament. A further meeting was planned at the Elephant public house, but unfortunately for the radicals news of this reached the notorious Deputy Constable of Manchester, Joseph Nadin. In a game of cat and mouse, the radical group reconvened at the Prince Regent's Arms in Ancoats to avoid the authorities, but despite this the meeting was interrupted and thirty-eight people were arrested.[5] This combination of politics and the pub proved to be a clear threat to social order, and the degree of concern amongst the authorities was such that legislation was introduced in 1817 to criminalise political gatherings in hostelries, and any breaches of the new law resulted in the forfeiture of publicans' licences.[6] The legislation placed responsibility for monitoring subversive activity firmly with publicans and innkeepers, and the threat of licence revocation against them was a vital means of social control.

The role of the *Manchester Observer*, the local radical newspaper during the earlier part of the century, was a key form of communication for working-class politics. The newspaper only lasted for two years, from 1818 to 1820, but was instrumental in creating a voice both for radical activists and indeed anyone who felt that they had been unjustly treated.[7] It was a newspaper the authorities were keen to suppress, particularly in pubs where newspapers were often read aloud to the illiterate in 'readings' that often took place to allow people to gain access to news and debate. However, whilst the newspaper provided a means of venting opinions, most did so anonymously. For example, one unknown Manchester publican, who was critical of the behaviour of some in authority, declared:

> I am a publican and have to complain of the many expenses which are heaped upon me, in common with my brethren, in obtaining a license. At present I shall only call your attention to a very singular one; it is that of 8s 2d, for what is called a certificate. I want to know of it be a legal fee; and if legal by what statute, we are, in a manner, thus plundered? Another matter worthy of some notice, is, that we are ordered to attend on Mr Nadin, at a public house *belonging to himself*, in order to give him this money, in which the clerk of the magistrates goes snacks with him. Our loss of money and time are not the only causes of just complaint. Nadin is so fond of Bank paper that though he may have plenty of silver on his table, he refuses to give change, with his usual for working-class politics *urbanity*. Whether the demand be legal or illegal, the mode of enforcing it, is, in my opinion, extremely improper. I am, Sir, if not an injured, an insulted publican.[8]

In fact, the *Manchester Observer* is one of the few sources of its kind in revealing grassroots opinions and radical political thinking, such was the undercover nature of their activity. The newspaper reported incidents of publicans being targeted for minor misdemeanours and occasionally having their licenses revoked in apparent retaliation for keeping the newspaper on their premises. It was reported how 'the publican is booked, and the first trivial circumstance on which he can be turned round upon commonly leads to dismissal from business'.[9] The printer and book seller James Wroe was one such person who had fallen foul of the authorities for selling the *Manchester Observer*, when in September 1819 his wife and their shop boy were arrested for selling a copy of the newspaper. James was already in prison at the time of incident and this was the second time his wife had been arrested. In 1820, James was further imprisoned for a year for selling a copy of *Sherwin's Political Register.*[10]

The Peterloo Massacre

Much of the political activity was inspired by the national leadership of the radical movement, Henry 'Orator' Hunt. Hunt was formerly a Wiltshire farmer, far removed from the role he was about to take on in pioneering northern working-class discontent, promoting parliamentary reform and providing the inspiration for the later Chartist movement that would continue the fight for further political reforms. Hunt was good at pulling in large northern crowds eager to listen to his radical messages and inspired people to challenge the government to implement much needed political reform, and it was such a meeting on St Peter's Field on 16 August 1819 that led to one of the most notable dates in Manchester's history. Starting with a seemingly carnival atmosphere, working-class processions came from the local towns – Oldham, Bury, Rochdale, Ashton-Under-Lyne and others – to convene on St Peter's Field to hear Orator Hunt's message about working-class political rights and the contentious issue of parliamentary reform.

34 Henry 'Orator' Hunt. (Courtesy of Alamy)

It was apparently a fine summer's day with, according to many eyewitnesses, a vibrant atmosphere, with groups flying banners and flags. Some were wearing white caps that had become a symbol of liberty, freedom and democracy. They all flocked to St Peter's Field to listen to Orator Henry Hunt. One of these was Samuel Bamford, who was quoted at the beginning of the chapter, who came in to Manchester that day with a group of people from his native Middleton. His eloquent description of the scene was within 10 minutes of the opening of the meeting. Bamford, a handloom weaver and radical, has left us a legacy of his life around Manchester, in his works, *Early Days* and *Passages in the Life of a Radical*. His quote at the beginning of the chapter has often been used since to capture the scene at Peterloo. In an apparent state of panic, the authorities sent in the Manchester and Cheshire Yeomanry Cavalry and Special Constables to control a crowd they argued were threatening and disorderly and required dispersal. However, witnesses in the crowd contradicted this, complaining of unnecessary violence as the cavalry charged in, slashing innocent people with their sabres. Some eyewitness accounts indicated that some of the officers were under the influence of alcohol. The cavalry, supported by a group of special constables, were certainly an ill-trained and poorly disciplined force. Many were volunteers from civilian professions, such as shopkeepers, publicans and manufacturers, and in fact publicans were a prominent occupational group, very likely fearing the loss of their licenses if they did not participate. John Ashworth of the Bull's Head Inn in Market Place was a special constable who was accidentally killed by the cavalry and reportedly 'sabred and trampled on'. Additionally, Thomas Redford, who was severely sabred on the shoulder, claimed he was 'cut by the young Oliver of the Swan-with-Two-Necks', referring to its landlord Andrew Oliver.[11] Further incidents took place immediately after the massacre, such as that which occurred in the New Cross area, where targets included publicans who had been special constables that day.[12] One of the more well-known victims of Peterloo was John Lees from Oldham, a 22-year-old who had served at the Battle of Waterloo and who later died from his sabre wounds. His inquest became a particularly notable event in attempting to uncover exactly what had happened. The initial location of his inquest, the Duke of York public house in Oldham, became inadequate for the publicity that the inquest received and it was relocated to the Star Inn in central Manchester. Henry Hunt and Samuel Bamford, amongst others, were

35 *Peterloo Massacre* by Richard Carlile. (Courtesy of Manchester Libraries, Information and Archives, Manchester City Council)

ST. PETER'S FIELDS
THE PETERLOO MASSACRE

On 16th August 1819 a peaceful rally
of 60,000 pro-democracy reformers,
men, women and children,
was attacked by armed cavalry
resulting in 15 deaths and
over 600 injuries.

116

36 Plaque commemorating the Peterloo Massacre on the Free Trade Hall building.

arrested and found guilty of treason in their involvement in Peterloo and were committed to Ilchester and Lincoln prisons.

The outcome is not open to debate, since fifteen were killed and hundreds injured in one of the most horrific acts against its own civilian population that this country has seen. What was more tragic was that there seemed little discrimination between those who were being maimed, with women and children also the subject of the troops' violence. Such was the seriousness of the events, the authorities implemented *Habeas Corpus*, detaining and imprisoning people without charge. Hugh Hornby Birley, captain of the Yeomanry Cavalry and a magistrate, lived in nearby Mosley Street, in a house overlooking St Peter's Field, and it was alleged that he ordered the reading of the riot act and gave orders to charge the crowd. It was said that feelings ran so high that at each anniversary of Peterloo radicals would meet opposite his house and groan.[13]

Radical Politics after Peterloo

The radical leadership reconsidered its tactics in the wake of events on St Peter's Field. This in itself was unsurprising, but what was alarming was their new policy of encouraging people to avoid the consumption of excisable products such as alcohol. The idea was to hit the government financially, and this strategy was voiced in the *Manchester Observer*, which reported:

> Touch not, taste not the unclean thing. The infernal powers that be will encourage public houses to sell that hellish liquor; to drink taxation; to make you mad, when you become an easy prey to their tyranny. Think and be wise.[14]

The focus was on boycotting public houses, which in theory would lead to a reduction in the payment of taxes on liquor, since according to the radical reformers, working-class payment of taxes on alcohol was 'contributing to their own enslavement'.[15] This was, in fact, an issue local radical and journalist Archibald Prentice observed only weeks prior to the Peterloo Massacre, who noted how the policy of abstaining from excisable products was coming to the forefront of radical political thinking in the Manchester region, with a meeting in June 1819 at St Peter's Field. Whilst the idea was already a potential alternative tactic in radical strategy, it was evident that the Peterloo Massacre led to this change. It was ironic that the authorities, who had at one time discouraged drinking to avoid people colluding in pubs and potentially creating social disorder, were now actively encouraging liquor consumption to counteract the effects of this new radical strategy. Prentice, in his recollections of Manchester politics at this time, highlights how the authorities were conveying this new drink message in Manchester's public houses, when he described how:

> A placard signed 'Bob Short', was stuck on all the walls, and distributed from house to house, denouncing all as enemies to the working people who would persuade them to renounce the use of the good old English drinks, and urging the readers to return to their good old drunken habits, to prove their attachment to King and Church Constitution, endangered by this conspiracy to promote sobriety.[16]

The radical leader, Henry Hunt, issued a message shortly after Peterloo which was blunt in conveying new radical tactics, which the *Manchester Observer* reported:

But above all, my friends, enter not the doors of a public house; refrain from all spirits and intoxicating liquors, remember that nine-tenths of the publicans are your enemies, they are tools in the hands of the Magistrates, and must do everything they wish them to do, however disgraceful, in order to secure their licenses. Abstain from beer, spirits and tea, and your health, your morals and character as men will be improved.[17]

However, it was a problem changing working-class habits. Ordinary working people who supported radicalism had their loyalty severely tested to a point that had the potential to undermine the foundations of the radical movement. Visiting the public houses for a drink was embedded in working-class culture and any change would not take place overnight. The 1820s was a relatively quiet decade for visible radical political action, but focused more on these other ways of influencing the authorities and parliamentarians of the need to extend voting rights.

Politics in the 1830s and 1840s

The 1830s began with renewed pressure on the government to recognise the rights of ordinary working people. During this time, working-class collaboration came in the form of a variety of meetings and processions. For example, in 1831 there was a procession through Manchester by the Working Class Union Movement, and it was reported in the local press that the gathering passed its regular meeting place, the King William the Fourth public house on Great Ancoats Street.[18] Also, the Manchester Political Tract Society held its first meeting at the Major Cartwright public house in New Cross in February 1834. The intention of this organisation was to diffuse political knowledge through the production of political tracts.[19] Despite the end of the *Manchester Observer* newspaper in 1820, the press continued to be a thorn in the side of the authorities, and sellers of the illegal 'unstamped' press were often at the wrong end of the law. One instance was that of the Oldham Street bookseller Abel Heywood, who in 1832 was imprisoned for four months for selling the unstamped *Poor Man's Guardian* and further fined in 1834 and 1836. John Doherty was an Irish radical who lived in Withy Grove, editing the *Voice of the People* then the *Poor Man's Advocate*. He was a social agitator and active in the passing of the Ten Hours Bill, and also suffered imprisonment for selling unstamped newspapers.[20]

In 1832, the Great Reform Act was passed. It was a pivotal piece of legislation designed to acknowledge places like Manchester that had no parliamentary representation up to this point. The results of the legislation were mixed, and the optimism that preceded it was not fulfilled in reality. It was disappointing to many mainly because it was not as far reaching as was hoped. Yes, more people could vote and Manchester gained two Members of Parliament, but the majority of these new voters were middle class, since voting rights were still based on male suffrage, and the amount of property one owned.[21] So the general election that took place in December 1832 was still minus working-class people. The Great Reform Act had some positive effects, since Manchester elected two MPs for the first time, Mark Philips and Charles Poulett Thomson. However, despite this there was still dissatisfaction that this legislation had not gone far enough. Some considered that it was the beginning of a more progressive democracy, yet others felt the legislation had just gone far enough to prevent a revolution without giving away too much. So, working-class groups reinforced their efforts to strive for further reforms. The result was Chartism.

The Chartist movement was a national organisation but its origins and presence were clearly felt in Manchester. Small localised Chartist meetings often took place in public houses, school rooms or trade society halls, which usually had an attached hostelry. Chartism was organised through a number of small localised branches, and Chartists meetings were often linked to trade and friendly societies, that also met in similar places, and Manchester contained around twelve Chartist districts.[22] For instance, the Queen's Stores public house in New Cross hosted the Tib Street district branch of the Chartists. The Mitre Inn at Hunt's Bank was noted as a friendly and familiar site, which also hosted meetings of the council of the Manchester Political Union (MPU) in the late 1830s.[24] The problem Chartists faced was where to meet, since in order to maintain credibility they tried to convene at places other than pubs, but when they attempted to hire municipal facilities such as the local town hall they were prevented from doing so.[25] Thus, pubs became the key place for not only local meetings but also for those of national standing too, but there were concerns amongst their ranks that this association with drink was losing their movement credibility, particularly amongst middle-class supporters of their cause, and casting doubt on its integrity amongst parliamentarians who were in a position of influence. Despite this, meetings continued wherever a venue could be found. For instance, a meeting took place at the Elephant public house on Tib Street, where about 250 people attended and one of the

Chartist leaders, Feargus O'Connor, spoke about the principles and objectives of the movement. The National Charter Association (NCA) of the Chartist movement emerged from a meeting held at the Griffin Inn on Great Ancoats Street.[26] Chartism had by now become a visible national movement which at the same time retained a strong regional focus.[27] The two-day event at the Griffin Inn was influential in organising every aspect of the movement's development, which included the formulation of policies, appointment of officers and administrators, and membership arrangements. The convention agreed to the implementation of a specific committee for overseeing the distribution of funds to families of imprisoned Chartists, which would be based in Manchester.[28] Furthermore, in March 1842, fifty-nine delegates met at the Hop Pole Inn to consider the means of securing the People's Charter, together with the abolition of the corn and provision laws.[29] In consequence, it is no surprise that some Mancunian publicans were active in their local Chartist movement. For instance, John Royle of the Town Hall Tavern was an elected member of the executive council of the Manchester Political Union and his pub was home of the Hulme and Chorlton-on-Medlock Chartists. R.J. Richardson and Edward Nightingale were also Chartist publicans.[30] In fact, Nightingale was landlord of the General Abercrombie tap rooms in Great Ancoats Street and was known to accommodate rough-house tactics at public meetings. He was active in both the New Cross and Ancoats areas of Manchester and organised gangs to invade meetings, especially those of the Anti-Corn Law League, though apparently he later repented his behaviour.[31] R.J. Richardson, a well-known radical figure in the Manchester and Salford area, was the secretary to the Manchester Political Union and had also been active in trade unionism and the anti-poor law movement.[32]

Middle-Class Politics

The middle class had their own political and economic interests to consider. As newfound wealth creators, they wanted a greater voice in Parliament and were concerned about protecting their trade and protecting their workforce to maintain productivity. Consequently, a number of ideologies and issues were vocalised. For instance, 'Manchester Men' were a group of prominent merchants and manufacturers who gained roles in politics and civic life at local and national levels. The 'Manchester School' developed an ideology of free trade and toward the emergence of the Anti-Corn Law League in response to food prices and its effects on working-class people.[33] Richard Cobden, a middle-class merchant and radical reformer, became a prominent figure in Manchester politics and became well known for two key issues. The first was his aim to make Manchester a modern municipal corporation, dispensing with its Lord of the Manor and feudal form of local government. Secondly, he was the driver behind the Anti-Corn Law League. The first of Cobden's objectives was to modernise how Manchester was governed. The 1835 Municipal Corporation Act was designed to implement a modern form of local government, by electing councillors and replacing the former system of unelected corporations. In 1838, Cobden began a campaign to free Manchester from its feudal form of local government and began to pressurise for a modern system of which Manchester was more worthy. He wrote a tract titled *Incorporate Your Borough – by a radical reformer*, which condemned the landed interest and agued how the middle class and 'industrious inhabitants' had built Manchester and needed to fight against the former privileged and aristocratic form of government. Manchester was by this time too large and too entrepreneurial to be restricted by such an antiquated form of governance. He was successful, and Manchester was indeed incorporated in 1838, ensuring that it was governed by a town council with appointed officials and greater accountability.

On 19 October 1837, a meeting was convened to discuss the reformation of local government, and where Richard Cobden and William Neild joined forces to develop a movement to pursue civic reform, at the manor court room in Brown Street.[34] Plans to reform local government had, in fact, begun in 1820 when a committee was assembled to plan for Manchester to receive a charter. However, officers changed every year, and this meant that progress was inhibited since no one was in office long enough to see through any changes. Nothing happened until 1832 when the Boroughreeve of the time, Benjamin Braidley, decided to pursue a more efficient form of policing. Progress was modest but some have seen this as a starting point in the process of local government reform. At national level, Lord Brougham introduced legislation which, whilst not going anywhere initially, did aim to improve systems of local government for towns that had become represented in Parliament after the Great Reform Act of 1832. In 1836, a meeting was convened to petition for a charter for Manchester, which William Neild chaired, but on this occasion the initiative was dropped. However, shortly after, during the brief time between the Court Leet session in October 1837 and the first public meeting of February 1838 in favour of incorporation, the decision to pursue the issue was finally made. Neild and Cobden were at the forefront of this campaign, and by this time Cobden had published his pamphlet *Incorporate Your Borough*.[35] Manchester had finally shaken off its feudal system and was being governed as a modern town should have been.

The year 1838 was also a key date for an entirely different reason, which led Cobden again to political prominence. During this time, Britain experienced particularly bad harvests and consequently food prices rose dramatically. The problem stemmed from the production of corn, or rather the inability to produce enough to feed the rapidly growing population. It meant that additional corn had to be imported. The government, in an attempt to protect farmers' interests, passed a corn law in 1815 to prohibit foreign corn being imported until domestic corn was over 80 shillings a quarter. This was a disaster on two fronts. First, it led to starvation and violence as people could not afford this most basic and staple food. Second, factory owners were not happy since their workforce was inefficient due to starvation and its effect on productivity, or they were faced with an increase in wages so their workforce could afford food. It also particularly affected Manchester since merchants could no longer carry on with their practice of exchanging textiles for corn. The Anti-Corn Law Association was convened in Manchester and first met at the York Hotel in King Street in September 1838. Richard Cobden was a leading advocate in this battle between the new entrepreneurial middle class versus the old out-of-date landed elites. It quickly became a national campaign, and by 1839 was supported by Robert Hyde Greg. The Greg family, residing at Styal, had become highly influential in local and national society, and had created a factory and model village for its workers in the Cheshire countryside, today known as Quarry Bank Mill. Robert also had a brief stint as a Manchester MP between 1839 and 1841. The government eased tariffs but did relatively little until 1845 when the weather ruined harvests and the potato famine had a devastating effect in Ireland. The level of deprivation and the threat to social order resulted in the corn laws being repealed in 1846. It meant that the working class could afford food again, as imports increased and prices fell. It was a defining moment for the middle class in challenging the government. They celebrated their success through the construction of the Free Trade Hall, which became symbolic of Manchester's middle-class men taking on the old fraternity and helping to create Manchester as a true modern city of the future. In 1867, a statue of Richard Cobden was erected in memory of his work connected with free trade.[36]

37 Statue of Richard Cobden in St Ann's Square.

Conclusion

This chapter has uncovered the conditions that working-class people endured as the industrial process began to radically affect Manchester, and the 'Shock City' of its age was turning political, fighting for better conditions and a voice in society. After all, those who were truly creating the wealth of the nation every day in the most appalling of conditions had no political say. This spilled over into discontent as the authorities and politicians of the time railed against change that would reduce their power. The result was Peterloo, the most notable date in Manchester's calendar, as the cavalry met protestors in the most violent of ways. Peterloo had a deep-rooted impact in society, which questioned how and why this state of affairs had arrived: what had gone wrong with society to create such issues, and what could be done about it? Working-class Mancunians were brave and not afraid to be political, and through their actions things improved slowly but surely. The working class were not the only prominent group challenging politics at national level, and there were clear middle-class voices that were also challenging the status quo. How did all of this play out later in the century? In the next chapter, the story continues throughout the 1840s and 1850s.

Notes

1   Swindells, *Manchester Streets*, vol. 1, p. 193.
2   de Tocqueville, A., *Journeys to England & Ireland* (Faber and Faber, 1958), pp. 107–8.
3   Faucher, *Manchester in 1844*, p. 19.
4   Kidd, *Manchester*, p. 77.
5   Prentice, *Historical Sketches*. pp. 76–8.
6   *The Statues, (Volume II), from the Eleventh Year of King George the Third to the First and second Years of King George the Fourth* (London, 3rd ed. 1950), pp. 702–3.
7   Belchem, J., 'Manchester, Peterloo and the Radical Challenge', *Manchester Region History Review*, vol. 3(1) (1989), pp. 9–14.
8   *Manchester Observer*, 19 September 1818.
9   *Manchester Observer*, 25 April 1818.
10 Swindells, *Manchester Streets*, vol. 1, p. 23.
11 Prentice, *Historical Sketches*, pp. 137, 167.
12 Bush, M., *The Casualties of Peterloo* (Carnegie, 2005), p. 39.
13 Swindells, *Manchester Streets*, vol. 1, p. 200.
14 *Manchester Observer*, 16 October 1819.
15 Vernon, J., *Politics and the People: A Study in English Political Culture, 1815–1867* (Cambridge University Press, 1993), p. 215.
16 Prentice, *Historical Sketches*, p. 150–1.
17 *Manchester Observer*, 23 October 1819.

18 *Manchester Times*, 7 May 1831.

19 *Poor Man's Guardian*, 15 February 1834.

20 Swindells, *Manchester Streets*, vol. 5, p. 103.

21 Evans, E., *The Great Reform Act of 1832* (Routledge, 1994), p. 45.

22 Pickering, P., *Chartism and the Chartists in Manchester* (Palgrave, 1995), p. 50; Chase, M., *Chartism: a new history (*Manchester University Press, 2007), p. 142.

23 Pickering, *Chartism*, p. 30; Chase, *Chartism*, p. 140–9.

24 Pickering, *Chartism*, pp. 1-30; *Northern Star*, 5 January 1839.

25 Pickering, *Chartism*, p. 30; Turner, 'Local Politics', p. 338.

26 Kidd, Manchester, p. 94.

27 Pickering, *Chartism*, p. 30.

28 *Northern Star*, 1 August 1840.

29 *Manchester Times*, 5 March 1842.

30 Pickering, *Chartism*, pp. 129–30.

31 Turner, 'Local Politics', p. 339, *Oxford Dictionary of National Biography* (http://www.oxforddnb.com)

32 Turner, 'Local Politics', p. 338.

33 Kidd, *Manchester*, p. 57.

34 Simon, *A Century*, p. 41.

35 Simon, *A Century*, pp. 71–80.

36 Swindells, *Manchester Streets*, vol. 1, p. 89.

six

ENGELS' MANCHESTER

I once went into Manchester with such a bourgeois, and spoke to him of the bad, unwholesome method
of building, the frightful condition of the working-peoples quarters, and asserted that I had never seen
so ill-built a city. The man listened quietly to the end, and said at the corner where we parted:
'And yet there is a great deal of money made here, good morning, sir.' It is utterly indifferent to
the English bourgeois whether his working-men starve or not, if only he makes money.

Friedrich Engels (1845)

Introduction

The industrial process altered the way the people of Manchester lived and
worked, and their place in society was governed by class. This chapter looks
at Manchester from the 1830s and examines how class shaped people's life
chances. It considers this through the eyes of one of the most critical observers and Marxist thinkers of his generation, Friedrich Engels. Engels, who
came to Manchester from Germany to manage the Weaste branch of the
family firm, *Herman and Engels*, was so moved by the way that urbanisation and industrialisation had overturned social norms and created a society
based on wealth and class that he produced his classic work *The Condition of
the Working Class in England* in 1845. Even though the title suggested it was
about England as a whole, in reality it was focused on Manchester. Here, he
emphasised how society at this time revolved around economic and social
distinction and hierarchy. His work has often received mixed reactions,
from those who see him accurately portraying the state of working-class
Manchester and its people, to others who focus on flaws in his observations,
inaccuracies and exaggeration to make a point. The original German ver-

sion was translated into English and some have concluded that some of his assertions may have been affected by this translation. His close links with Karl Marx provided him with a distinctly socialist political perspective, and his critics took him to task for fitting his ideology around his observations rather than adopting a more objective approach. Despite the shortcomings of his work, Engels' book is still an iconic piece of history that is discussed and debated in classrooms. So what is it that has kept this work at the heart of debate on Manchester's nineteenth-century history? The quote opening the chapter emphasises what was both wrong and right with society at this time. Manchester was a global powerhouse of industry and wealth creation, but with an unfortunate downside, although is this not always the case with success? Here, we were at the epicentre of industrial life, where wealth was being created on a monumental scale, but it was still a place forging a modern outlook from backward practices and divisions in the way people lived and worked. The chapter will show how the working class worked and lived, by looking at work they did, their housing, recreation and crime. This is contrasted with middle-class life and politics, whose aspirations and moral codes differed markedly from those of working-class people, with their focus on respectability and 'separate sphere' gender divisions.

Working-Class Life

What was working-class life really like? For one thing, the pressure of population had rapidly increased. In 1801, the first proper census, it is estimated that Manchester contained around 95,000 people and by 1831 this had risen to around 187,000, and by 1851, 316,000.[1] Much of this was due to migration to the area, not just from surrounding towns and villages, but importantly from across the waters where the Irish, who were suffering the consequences of unemployment and the potato famine from the mid-1840s, came to places like Liverpool and Manchester to find work. Many of the Irish who came to Manchester settled around an area created by a bend in the river Medlock, in Chorlton-on-Medlock, close to the current Oxford Road railway station. It became known as 'Little Ireland' and was one of the poorest places in the city. A local doctor, J.P. Kay, who worked in nearby Ancoats, had witnessed at close quarters the deprivation and disease that had become commonplace. In his 1832 report, *The Moral and Physical Condition of the Working Classes Employed in the Cotton Manufacture in Manchester*, which he produced after a particularly bad outbreak of cholera, he describes the area around Little Ireland:

> A portion of low swampy ground, liable to be frequently inundated, and to constant exhalation, is included between a high bank over which the Oxford Road passes, and a bend of the river Medlock, where its course is impeded by weirs. This unhealthy spot lies so low that the chimneys of its houses, some of them three stories high, are a little above the level of the road. About 200 of these habitations are crowded together in an extremely narrow space, and are inhabited by the lowest Irish. Most of these houses have also cellars, whose floor is scarcely elevated above the level of the water flowing in the Medlock. The soughs are destroyed or out of repair: and these narrow abodes are in consequence always damp, and the slightest rise in the river, which is a frequent occurrence, are flooded to the depth of several inches. The district has been frequently the haunt of hordes of thieves and desperadoes who defied the law, and is always inhabited by a class resembling savages in their appetites and habits. It is surrounded on every side by some of the largest factories of the town, whose chimney vomit forth dense clouds of smoke, which hang heavily over this insalubrious region.[2]

Just over ten years later, little had changed, and Engels provided a vivid account of the same area:

> The stretch cut through by the Birmingham railway is the most thickly built-up and worst. Here flows the Medlock with countless windings through a valley of the Irk. Along both sides of the stream, which is coal black, stagnant, and foul, stretches a broad belt of factories and working-men's dwellings, the latter all in the worst condition. The bank is chiefly declivitous and is built over to the water's edge, just as we saw along the Irk, while the houses are equally bad, whether built on the Manchester side or in Ardwick, Chorlton or Hulme. But the most horrible spot (if I should describe all the separate spots in detail I should never come to the end) lies on the Manchester side, immediately south-west of Oxford Road, and is known as Little Ireland. In a rather deep hole, in a curve of the Medlock and surrounded on all four sides by tall factories and high embankments, covered with buildings, stand two groups if about two hundred cottages built chiefly back to back, in which live about four thousand human beings, most of them Irish. The cottages are old and dirty, and of the smallest sort, the streets uneven, fallen into ruts and in part without drains of pavement; masses of refuse, offal and sickening filth lie among the standing pools in

all directions; the atmosphere is poisoned by the effluvia from these, and laden and darkened by the smoke of a dozen tall factory chimneys. A horde of ragged women and children swarm about here, as filthy as the swine that thrive upon the garbage heaps and in the puddles. In short, the whole rookery furnishes such a hateful and repulsive spectacle as can hardly be equalled in the worst court on the Irk.[3]

The conditions the poorest people in Manchester, including the Irish immigrants, lived in had a profound effect on their health, and a report of the Poor Law Commission in 1842 estimated that 57 per cent of the 'labouring class' died before the age of 5 years.[4] Before the Irish potato famine in 1841, the Irish made up around 12 per cent of Manchester's population, rising to 13 per cent around 1851. J.P. Kay was less than flattering about the Irish in Manchester, suggesting that they had brought some bad habits that were having a detrimental effect on the locals. However, he failed to acknowledge that Irish immigrants faced some of the worst deprivation. In his report Kay stated that: 'the colonization of the Irish was thus first encouraged; and had proved one chief source of demoralization, and consequent physical depression of the people'.[5] There were an estimated 35,000 to 40,000 Irish in Manchester, and they were often the poorest and most unhealthy, and were seen as the perpetrators of crime, theft and more serious offences. Whilst it was not an exclusive problem, drink was seen as a problem amongst the Irish, though through support by the Catholic Church many were cutting their drink habits and even taking the temperance pledge, and this was seen to reduce crime and disorder.[6]

Prior to 1868 there was little legislation to control the construction and quality of housing. Consequently, houses were thrown together, often back-to-back, many with cellar dwellings and with no sanitation, running water or any other basic provision. This resulted in incredibly unhealthy conditions rife with disease. The increase in population led to an endless housing shortage and the dwellings available were hastily or 'jerry built' terraces on whatever land was available. Most were single-course brick with several large families living in a very small space. Cellars were the cheapest, and here they could house around twenty people in a single cellar dwelling. Engels provides an insight into the worst of conditions:

Right and left a multitude of covered passages lead from the main street into numerous courts and he who turns hither gets into a filth and disgusting grime, the equal of which is not to be found, especially in the courts which lead down to the Irk and

38 Friedrich Engels in 1845, aged 25. (Courtesy of Alamy)

which contain unqualifiedly the most horrible dwellings which I have yet beheld. In one of these courts there stands directly at the entrance, at the end of the covered passage, a privy without a door, so dirty that the inhabitants can pass into and out of the court only by passing through foul pools of stagnant urine and excrement'.[7]

It was not quite the same experience for the middle class who were moving away from the original high-class residential areas of Mosley Street, George Street, and Faulkner Street. By the 1830s, they were moving out to the new residential suburbs of south Manchester and Pendleton. The houses they left behind were increasingly being taken over by warehousing, and the people who were replacing them in the centre led to higher rates of poverty and vice. Contemporary observer Leon Faucher, who wrote *Manchester in 1844: its present condition and future prospects,* stated:

The rich man spreads his couch amidst the beauties of the surrounding country, and abandons the town to the operatives, publicans, mendicants, thieves and prostitutes merely taking the precaution to leave behind him a police force, whose duty it is to preserve some little of material order in this pell-mell of society.[8]

However, despite this overwhelmingly gloomy picture, the situation for the working-class started to improve. From the 1830s and '40s there were a number of factory acts that dealt with issues such as the employment of children and limits to working hours. In 1844, legislation was passed that ensured that all new houses had a water supply and either an indoor or outdoor toilet. Cellar dwellings in Manchester ceased after legislation passed in 1853 and several hundred were demolished.

Manchester's authorities were faced with increases in crime and social problems in consequence of urbanisation and concentrations of very poor people in working-class districts. One of the most contentious issues for the authorities to deal with was the working-class association with drink and pubs. Even though working-class people endured gruelling days, they made the most of their free time, which was often in their local hostelry. Manchester had in the region of 500 public houses around this time, so there were plenty of places to choose from. Furthermore, from 1830 the drink question became a pressing issue owing to the Beer Act of that year which transformed drink culture in places such as Manchester since it allowed anyone with a few guineas to obtain an excise license and open a beerhouse that, as its name implies, sold just beer. These beerhouses proliferated all over the city to well over a thousand, particularly in working-class districts such as Hulme, Newton Heath, Ancoats, and neighbouring Salford.[9]

One of Manchester's most famous policemen was Detective Jerome Caminada, and his memoirs offers us fascinating insights into the less salubrious aspects of Mancunian life, and often incidents revolved around pubs and beerhouses. Born in Deansgate to an Irish mother and Italian father, Jerome was brought up in the area noted for its criminal underworld and vice during the nineteenth century. He began work at the police force in 1868, and soon developed through the ranks, becoming a detective in 1872. He was prolific in his investigations and convicted thousands of people and closed down hundreds of pubs and beerhouses down during his career. His two-volume memoirs – *25 Years of Detective Life* – provide colourful accounts of some of the cases he dealt with. He gave us invaluable insights into life inside a working-class pub, citing:

Passing these the pedestrian's ear would be arrested by the sound of music proceeding from mechanical organs, accompanied sometimes with drums and tambourines. On entering the premises he would find a number of youths and girls assembled in a room furnished with a few wooden forms and tables. The women generally lived upon the premises, the proprietor of the den often adding to his income by the proceedings of their shame. Some rude attempt would probably be made at an indecent song by a half-drunken girl for the edification of some collier lads, who were the chief victims of these haunts, but their voice would be drowned by the incessant quarrelling and obscene language of her companions.[10]

Another policeman who left us with an account of his life and work was Superintendent James Bent, whose memoirs, *Crime Life*, add to our understanding of criminal activity at this time. Bent recalled an incident in which he attended a beerhouse in Newton Heath where a false wall had been constructed which, on removal, revealed a bedroom that had been fitted out with a bar to sell out-of-hours alcohol. This beerhouse did not remain open for very long after Bent's discovery.[11] There were a whole range of recreations that developed around drink culture, and the type of leisure pursuits on offer differed according to the type of hostelry. Both pubs and beerhouses put on musical entertainment, and customers enjoyed playing dominoes and cards, and sometimes the resulting gambling led to conflicts with the law. Beerhouses were particularly known for 'lower' forms of recreation that included very basic forms of music and dancing, gaming and gambling, cruel sports such as dog-fighting, and prostitution.[12]

Pubs offered a range of activities. Newspapers were a common feature in pubs, where customers consulted the latest news and read aloud to illiterate customers. Writer and observer William Cooke-Taylor, when touring the region, noted that newspapers were the main attraction in pubs, particularly on a Sunday.[13] The accessibility and readership of a newspaper in a pub far exceeded its actual circulation, providing both a social function in keeping people abreast of current affairs and, as we saw earlier, it was a means of keeping up with political news.[14] Poetry was a popular pastime and pubs provided an outlet for those with literary tastes, and again we saw earlier how the Sun Inn in Long Millgate hosted a local 'Poet's Corner' where the likes of Peterloo veteran Samuel Bamford, Elijah Ridings and other literary specialists often met to recite their works.[15] The Sun Inn Group, as they were commonly known, became famous at both local and national level, and whilst they were never regarded as critically acclaimed poets they showed an aspect of working-class culture that reveals that it was not just about the doom and gloom of factory life, poor conditions and lack of education, but a vibrant and artistic culture that prevailed. Local botanical societies often met in pubs, where meeting rooms and space for libraries were paid for by purchases of alcohol and there was usually a membership fee which covered club costs plus drink. The Golden Lion on Rochdale Road was one such pub that hosted a local botanical society, and on one occasion in 1858 it was reported that over thirty societies and some 200 people attended a botanical event hosted there.[16] Friendly societies were also commonplace in pubs, where members could pay a nominal amount to cover them for sickness, unemployment and burial costs in the event of death, thus providing a vital service until the introduction of formal national insurance contributions. Manchester was home to a good number of societies and became the originator of one of the most notable friendly societies in the Manchester Unity Order of Oddfellows.[17]

One of the most popular working-class pastimes was music, and musical entertainment took a number of forms, from informal singing through to the development of more formalised musical and theatrical-style entertainment. Music such as the 'free and easy' session, where many would sing along to someone at the piano, was a simple pleasure for many which was enjoyed at their local pub or beerhouse, and it was out of this tradition that more formalised entertainment emerged. Publicans became proficient at staging amusements that included musical hall acts, amateur talent nights and free and easy sessions, and quite often aspiring professional singers used free and easy sessions for practice to gain careers in the emerging music halls, which began to offer more professional musical entertainment.[18] The traditional local amateur entertainment of the pub and the free and easy became more specialised, where back-room informal get-togethers turned into a singing saloon style of concerts with expanded premises and professional performers.[19] Music saloons began to appear in pubs as, from the 1830s, publicans began to create concert rooms, and some of these turned into larger music halls, often housing 1,000 people.[20] Some of Manchester's most notable music halls included the Casino, the Victoria, and Polytechnic Hall whose combined audiences averaged 25,000 each week, and the majority of these were young working-class lads. The most popular night was Friday, particularly if this was pay day.[21]

Outdoor recreation was popular amongst a working-class that had been enduring the factory for most of the week. Manchester is not traditionally associated with horse racing, but it was a popular pastime during the eighteenth and nineteenth centuries at Kersal Moor races, which began in 1730. It was a very popular venue for all classes of people in and around the area, and was in operation for over a hundred years but ended in 1847.[22] Another popular working-class leisure venue was Belle Vue, which opened its gates in May 1837. Belle Vue was one of the region's most popular venues for outdoor recreation until well into the twentieth century. It was located on Hyde Road in Longsight and owned by John Jennison, and remained in the family for over a hundred years. John Jennison was born in 1790 and started out his working life as a Macclesfield silk weave, but he also had a passion for gardening and he decided to pursue work in horticulture. He married Maria Barber in 1826 and their sons eventually took over the control of Belle Vue. Jennison was interested in gardening and he had also managed to collect a great number of unusual birds that included parrots, macaws, cockatoos, gold and silver pheasants, peacocks of different descriptions and swans, as well as a variety of animals. His success as a gardener was such that he opened part of it up on a Sunday for people to visit. He later added wildlife and it became famously known as Jennison's garden. He eventually moved to the Belle Vue site and developed a zoological as well as botanical gardens. Unfortunately, the site had a chequered history and suffered financial difficulties several times. In 1842, Jennison faced bankruptcy but due to the lack of a sale and the closure of nearby competitor, Manchester Zoological Gardens, his creditors gave him another chance and from here the park developed into a serious visitor attraction.

Middle-Class Life

Life for the working-class people of Engels' Manchester was tough but at the same time they enjoyed their limited free time. Life was very different for the middle class, who were prominent in the cultural life of Manchester, enjoying and promoting both the arts and sciences through a number of clubs and organisations they established, often financed by private subscription. Middle-class life revolved around one key theme, that of moral Victorian respectability. Men and women had distinct roles in society, or 'separate spheres' as they were often referred to, where men were the breadwinners and women looked after their homes, though in reality many middle-class women had domestic servants to assist them and many, due to boredom and lack of a purposeful role, engaged in charitable work. One such woman was the novelist Elizabeth Gaskell, who settled in Manchester with her husband, the Cross Street Chapel Unitarian minister, William Gaskell. In line with many middle-class women of her day, Elizabeth had a full life in caring for her family and the household, and supported numerous charities, most notably helping the poor and children. The Gaskells were very much tapped into the cultural and intellectual life of middle-class Manchester, being prominent in the Literary and Philosophical Society and the Athenaeum, though Elizabeth's role here was limited as a middle-class woman in a very middle-class male world. Instead, Elizabeth channelled her observations into her novels. One of her key works about the struggles of Manchester working-class life was *Mary Barton*, published in 1848. Here, she wrote at the height of Chartism, which features prominently in this novel, and it was a controversial read at the time, provoking debate on the condition of working Manchester. It was here that she attracted the attention of Charles Dickens, and despite their often tenuous relationship he showed great interest and support for her work. She was very much connected to the literary talents of the day and boasted of friendships with other notable literary specialists including the Brontës, John Ruskin and Thomas Carlyle. Other novels she produced included *Cranford*, *North and South* and *Wives and Daughters*. The family took up residence at Dover Street, now located on the University of Manchester's campus just off Oxford Road. They later moved to Plymouth Grove and it is here that her former residence became a museum in her memory.[23] Gaskell, in contrast to Engels, portrayed Manchester working life in a literary context, yet was similar to Engels in conveying to the reader what life was like for many local factory workers and the difficulties they faced.

Through her novel, *Mary Barton*, Gaskell conveyed a tale of Manchester life between 1839 and 1842, at the height of depression and Chartism. Mary Barton, daughter of John Barton who becomes a Chartist and trade unionist, felt the need to marry the mill owner's son, Harry Carson, instead of her working-class childhood sweetheart, Jem, in order to try and secure a decent future for the family. However, things turned out very differently in this tale of the classes breaking their boundaries. Additionally, *North and South* emphasises the distinction between the two halves of the country, as Margaret Hale moves from London to 'Milton', an imaginary place in the north, dirty and filled with poverty, which Margaret struggles to adapt to but then finds a comfort and strength in the working-class plight she experiences. Again, it is a tale of mill owner versus workers, and a blossoming romance between Margaret and mill

39 Elizabeth Gaskell in her later years.

owner Mr Thornton, struggling with the moral dilemmas of the way the middle class treat their workers, strike action and the huge chasm between the classes.

Middle-class men engaged in a social life that was designed to promote their status as an economic and moral force. They did not grace public houses, unless of course it was a respectable inn, and networking revolved around a number of arts and science institutions that were paid for by private subscription. These included the Athenaeum, the Royal Institution, the Portico and the Literary and Philosophical Society. In particular, many were Unitarians and attended Cross Street Chapel where William Gaskell was a minister, and here notable middle-class families such as the Potters, Abel Heywood, and J.P. Kay were in the congregation and held civic office at one time or another.[24] The Manchester Athenaeum for the diffusion of knowledge, the idea originating from surgeon John Walker, began at a meeting at the York Hotel in 1835 and was designed for 'intellectual cultivation' with reading and news rooms, a library and a regular lecture series. In 1839, it had managed to raise enough funds to open its own building on Princess Street, and there were in the region of 1,000 subscribers.[25] Many annual soirees were held, including one hosted by Charles Dickens in 1843 and Benjamin Disraeli in 1844. However, despite support from some of the most well known in society, the 1840s was a particularly tough time financially and the club almost ended before it had truly begun.[26] However, it did survive and attracted at least 1,400 members, offered lectures, a 6,000-volume library, language study and elocution lessons. Subscibers could also partake in music and other rational pleasures, such as poetry readings and recitals by notable writers.[27] The Royal Manchester Institution for the Promotion of Literature, Science and the Arts was established in 1823. George Wood, a prominent Manchester merchant, was the brainchild behind the proposal to set up such an institution and who first called a meeting to raise subscriptions, and by 1824 £23,000 had been raised. The Manchester Royal Institution building was designed by prominent architect Charles Barry, and cost around £30,000 to build. Construction work began in 1829 and was completed in 1834. It had space for exhibitions, paintings, and a theatre for lectures.[28] It had already started its acquisitions before the building was complete, purchasing James Northcote's study of the black actor Ira Aldridge, 'Othello, The Moor Of Venice', in 1827. Its focus was on art and sculpture and to encourage literary and scientific and artistic interests, and an annual exhibition of paintings was held there. It was well supported and included the Duke of Wellington as one of its patrons, and the institution was instrumental in supporting the Art Treasures exhibition of 1857.[29] Its galleries opened to the public from the 1830s, but despite it technically being open to everyone, in reality many working-class people could not afford the entrance fee, which created a barrier to access. By the early 1880s, the building and contents became part of Manchester Corporation, and became Manchester Art Gallery. In 1880, finances were tight and it was decided to incorporate it into Manchester Council, which agreed to provide £2,000 each year for twenty years to purchase artwork.[30]

The Literary and Philosophical Society (or Lit and Phil) began at a meeting in George Street in 1781, and was seen as a way for the new urban rich elite

40　Manchester Art Gallery.

to establish and flaunt their newfound status. Initially, there were in the region of 150 members, including the notable scientist John Dalton, who became president for a time. The society published transactions, some of which were scientific in nature, and included Dalton's atomic theory. The society comprised ordinary, honorary and corresponding members, and all members had to demonstrate their publication credentials, and entry to the society relied on the prospective member acquiring references from three ordinary members. The Portico was an independent subscription reading room and library designed for leading merchants and gentlemen.[31] Also on Mosley Street and close to the Art Gallery, it was financed through private subscription and opened in 1806. Its facilities included a library, bar, committee room and news room. By 1834, the library contained around 9,000 volumes and had around 400 subscribers.[32]

The middle class of Manchester were good at displaying their wealth in this array of cultural and scientific institutions. However, they were equally concerned about the condition of the working class. Some would regard this as an attempt to show genuine concern for helping their employees and for their welfare. Others considered it a cynical attempt to impose a moral code on a class to maintain social order and raise standards. Either way, the middle class were heavily involved in schemes to educate and provide moral guidance to a class that was deemed uneducated and had to be diverted away from recreation that involved pubs and drink. An example of this intervention came in the form of the Sunday school movement which began in Manchester in 1784. This flourished, and some forty years later around 23,000 children were being educated through Sunday schools, largely financed by the middle class.[33] A number of middle-class initiatives aimed at working people started to emerge between the late 1820s and the 1850s that were collectively coined 'rational recreation'. These included the provision of libraries, parks and Mechanics' Institutes. One of the first initiatives that the middle class invested in was that of the Mechanics' Institutes. In 1824, William Fairbairn, Thomas Hopkins and Richard Roberts came up with the idea of developing an educational institution. At a meeting at the Bridgewater Arms inn chaired by Benjamin Heywood, they lobbied for an institution that would offer lectures, libraries and other educational recreation for working-class people. The first that opened in the area was in 1825, with many receiving a basic education in writing, reading and maths. The first Mechanics' Institute was built in Cooper Street, with finance raised by shares, and opened in March 1825. By the 1830s, attendance was declining, so more social events were put on to turn this around.[34] For a nominal subscription of 5 shillings a quarter, members could attend evening classes, libraries and reading rooms. They became popular for self-improvement, and in 1838, for example, there were 1,161 members, with ages ranging from 14 years upwards.[35] In 1834, a boys' school was opened, followed by a school for girls. By 1842, there

41 The Portico Library.

were 1,300 members, contributing £1 each per annum. A second building was opened in 1857 on Princess Street. Lyceums were another similar kind of institution and in 1838 lyceums were opened in Ancoats, Chorlton-on-Medlock and Salford, offering a similar form of education as the Mechanics' Institutes.[36]

Manchester established the first public free library in the country. Of course, Manchester had always had a library that technically was freely available in Chetham's library, that was originated by Humphrey Chetham in 1653. Chetham's library comprised around 25,000 volumes and was available to all, and was one of the best collections in the country. However, its location and seclusion kept it away from the prying eyes of the community at large, so in reality it was not treated as an open-access library.[37] The free public library movement in Manchester opened the first public free library in 1852 in Campfield near Deansgate. It greatly expanded the range of publications on offer to people who had previously relied on Mechanics' Institutes and other such places for materials to read.[38] In 1851, Edward Edwards was appointed as the first librarian following the Public Libraries Act. An inaugural ceremony of the new library at Campfield was in September 1852, attended by the literary giants Charles Dickens and William Thackray.

In 1833, the Select Committee on Public Walks paved the way for the introduction of parks and recreational public spaces, in particular to provide open spaces for working-class recreation that were deemed respectable and healthy pursuits. The Select Committee was the catalyst for Manchester to try to solve the problem of working-class recreation by diverting them towards more wholesome leisure pursuits and away from drink. Four prominent Mancunians gave evidence to the committee, notably Benjamin Braidley, Richard Potter, Joseph Brotherton, and Mark Philips, and they all came to the conclusion that there was a need for this kind of facility. It was a largely middle-class initiative, by which not only was it seen as a healthier recreation, but that the working-class were supposed to see how the middle-class behaved and dressed in a way that would cascade down moral and social codes of behaviour. By the mid-1840s, papers such as the *Manchester Guardian* were promoting the notion of a lack of publicly available outdoor space and the need for public parks. By this time, many of the middle class had moved to the suburbs, creating further voids in the city centre, increasing the potential for working-class vice after a gruelling day in the factory. Whilst the concept of a pleasure garden was nothing new, with Pomona Gardens in Hulme and Belle Vue offering outdoor leisure, these venues did not concur with middle-class views on respectability. By August

1844, the first meeting to discuss the implementation of a parks initiative was organised. But it was a middle-class affair, mainly comprising of Liberal reformers. Finance was raised via subscription and this proved very popular, since by March 1845 over £30,000 had been generated. The first public park to open was Peel Park in Salford, where Lark Hill estate was purchased to develop the land into a public space. Hendham Hall in Harpurhey became Queen's Park and land acquired from Lady Houghton in Bradford became Philips Park, and named after one of the advocates of the public parks scheme, Mark Philips MP. These three parks all opened at the same time in August 1846.[39]

Conclusion

Life in Engels' Manchester was one of great contrasts between rich and poor, the haves and have nots, and this was played out in every aspect of daily life. Working-class life was hard. The long hours, working and living conditions were demanding, yet this situation began to improve. A series of legislation began to improve different aspects of the quality of life. The middle class were a prominent part of Manchester's culture, and they invested in a range of institutions to display their wealth and status. They also made attempts to improve working-class life but there are differing interpretations of their motivations for these acts of philanthropy. The time up to the 1850s had been one of economic, political and social turbulence, but as we move beyond mid-century there begins a settling in society, and this is the focus of the next chapter.

Notes

1 (1831) The Complete Account of the Population of Great Britain (348), and (1901) Census of England and Wales [Cd.616], *House of Commons Parliamentary Papers;* Kidd, *Manchester,* p. 14.

2 Kay, Shuttleworth J., *The Moral and Physical Condition of the Working Classes Employed in the Cotton Manufacture in Manchester* (James Ridgeway, 1832), pp. 21–2.

3 Engels, F., *The Condition of the Working Class in England,* translated by W.O. Henderson & W.H. Chaloner (Blackwell, 1845 (1958)), pp. 93–4.

4 Simon, *A Century,* p. 166.

5   Kay, *The Moral and Physical Condition*, pp. 21–50.

6   Faucher, *Manchester in 1844*, p. 30.

7   Engels, *The Condition*, p. 82.

8   Faucher, *Manchester in 1844*, pp. 26–7.

9   See Woodman, D., *The Public House in Manchester and Salford, c 1815–1880* (PhD thesis, Leeds Metropolitan University, 2011) for more on this topic.

10 Caminada, J., *25 Years of Detective Life in Victorian Manchester*, vol. 2 (1895), p. 16.

11 Bent, J., *Criminal Life: Reminiscences of Forty-Two Years as a Police Officer* (John Heywood, 1891), p. 153.

12 *Manchester Times*, 9 July 1853.

13 Cooke Taylor, *Notes of a Tour in the Manufacturing Districts of Lancashire* (Duncan & Malcolm, 1842), p. 136; Rose, J., *The Intellectual Life of the British Working Classes* (Yale University Press, 2001), p. 84.

14 Rose, *The Intellectual Life,* p. 84.

15 Swindells, *Manchester Streets*, vol. 4, pp. 72–3.; *Manchester Times*, 4 September 1880.

16 Swindells, *Manchester Streets,* vol. 5, p. 173.

17 Gosden, P., *The Friendly Societies in England, 1815-1875* (Manchester University Press, 1961); Cordery, S., *British Friendly Societies, 1750-1914* (Palgrave, 2003).

18 Poole, R., *Wakes Holidays and Pleasure Fairs in the Lancashire Cotton District, c.1790–1890* (PhD thesis, Lancaster University, 1985), p. 159; Free Lance, 2 March 1867.

19 Bailey, P., *Music Hall: the business of pleasure* (Open University Press, 1991), p. ix.

20 Poole, R., *Popular Leisure and the Music Hall in Nineteenth Century Bolton* (Centre for North-West Regional Studies, 1982), p. 51; Kift, D., *The Victorian Music Hall: culture, class and conflict* (Cambridge University Press, 1996); Russell, *Popular Music in England 1840–1914: a social history* (Manchester University Press, 1997), p. 26.

21 Kift, *The Victorian Music Hall*, pp. 1–2, 71.

22 Love, *Manchester*, p. 143.

23 gaskellsociety.co.uk

24 Simon, *A Century*, p. 32.

25 Love, *Manchester*, p. 100.

26 Swindells, *Manchester Streets*, vol. 2, p. 32.

27 *Manchester Times*, 30 December 1843.

28 Everett, *Panorama of Manchester*, p. 220.

29 Love, Manchester, p. 110; Everett, *Panorama of Manchester*, p. 229.

30 Simon, *A Century*, pp. 274.

31 Love, *Manchester*, p.111, 191–2.

32 Everett, *Panorama of Manchester*, p. 219.

33 Simon, *A Century*, p. 212.

34 Kidd, *Manchester*, p. 51.

35 Love, *Manchester*, p. 102.

36 Swindells, *Manchester Streets*, vol. 2, pp. 39–44.

37 Love, *Manchester*, p. 127.

38 Kidd, *Manchester*, p. 52.

39 Wyborn, T., 'Parks for the People: the development of public parks in Victorian Manchester, *Manchester Region History Review*, vol. 9 (1995), pp. 3–14.

seven

STABILITY OF THE MIDDLE YEARS

What Art was to the ancient world, Science is to the modern: the distinctive faculty.
In the minds of men the useful has succeeded to the beautiful. Instead of the city of the Violet
Crown, a Lancashire village has expanded into a mighty region of factories and warehouses.
Yet rightly understood, Manchester is as great a human exploit as Athens.

Benjamin Disraeli, Coningsby (1844)

Introduction

Manchester's start to the nineteenth century was turbulent. Changes in life, work and politics had been swift and people of all classes in society had struggled to keep up with the pace of change. The second half of the nineteenth century was much quieter in this respect, and society appears to have settled. The economy became more stable, and whilst not all had been achieved politically, there was at least some progress in the ultimate working-class aim of voting rights and democracy. It was during this time that Manchester came of age. The Collegiate Church became Manchester Cathedral in 1847, but it was ironic that this did not immediately convey city status. This came on 2 April 1853, when Manchester finally became a city. As the local newspaper, *Manchester Courier*, pointed out, it was an odd intervening five years for Manchester, for as big and important as it was, Manchester was effectively a 'Cathedral Town'.[1] Finally, Manchester gained the status it deserved and displays of this new status of wealth and industry were articulated in a number of ways. One of the most spectacular examples was that of the Art Treasures Exhibition of 1857, which was one of the most flagrant displays of art, culture, and science ever seen in this country. Civic pride emerged in the form of a new town hall with an architecture that reflected Manchester's newfound status. There were also engineering endeavours on an unprecedented scale that were to transform trade through, for example, the construction of the Manchester Ship Canal and the emergence of a transport system fit for a modern global city. Politics? Well, the 1867 Reform Act extended the limitations of the Great Reform Act of 1832, and further legislation in the 1880s ensured a more settled and progressive democracy that even the working men of Manchester could enjoy. Though what about women? It is during this era of Victorian stability that women began to air their political voice and challenge for equality and proper democratic rights. Finally, there was the emergence of a consumer culture that heralded the arrival of some lavish department stores whose names remain familiar even today.

The Mid-Victorian City

During the mid-Victorian period Manchester's population had risen from around 316,000 in 1851 and to 462,000 by 1881, so whilst this was a clear increase, the rate had steadied, though Manchester remained the largest concentration of population outside London.[2] The city was changing, since where there had once been areas of working-class slums filled with vice, such as parts of Deansgate, Oldham Road, Angel Meadow and the areas close to Rochdale Road that were especially notorious for drunkenness and crime, from the 1850s slum clearance in central Manchester removed around 13,000 people, including the areas around Market Street, Deansgate and London Road, which were subject to street widening and redevelopment.[3] The middle class had already moved away from the centre some time before, and the space they left behind had become left open for working-class vice to move in, occupying the slum areas of Angel Meadow, Little Ireland and parts of Deansgate close to Spinningfield. However, by the mid-century even these areas were changing and were being cleaned up and becoming commercial and shopping spaces. Working-class people were also migrating out of the city centre and, in fact, were now occupying spaces that the middle class had originally occupied before moving further out into newer wealthy suburbs, resulting in once middle-class affluent areas such as Ardwick on the immediate periphery of the city centre being taken up with poorer housing. Where Mosley Street had once been the place where

Manchester's rich lived, it was by now a thriving centre for warehousing as the commercial class moved out to live in places such as Withington and Didsbury and even parts of Cheshire. The development of road and rail transport during the 1830s and 1840s had given them the scope to live in the outer suburbs and commute into the city each day. The development of Withington and Didsbury followed the Oxford road corridor in a ribbon development of more sumptuous terraces and villas through Fallowfield. These areas were largely absent of factories and gave opportunity for leafy suburbs to emerge, unlike places such as east Manchester, which always retained a working-class character owing to the industry that had grown there. Residential parks emerged as a distinctive feature of middle-class housing areas to effectively ring fence them. One of the first examples of this was Victoria Park, which emerged around 1837 and provided almost a country-retreat existence for those that could afford to live there, and it was still a desirable place to live well into the twentieth century.

The development of transport was one of the factors that enabled the growth of suburbs around Manchester, and by the early 1850s transport had become a more organised and far-reaching network, both by road and rail. The expansion of railway lines radiating out from central Manchester to places such as Altrincham and Wilmslow provided lines of affluent housing where middle-class people could easily commute into Manchester each day. By the 1860s, middle-class residential areas were springing up in Cheshire, such as Alderley Edge and Bowden, as rail travel became more advanced. Sale and Streford grew alongside the line to Altrincham. Cheadle, Bramhall and Heaton Moor grew alongside the Wilmslow line. By the 1870s, lines to Warrington and Bury encouraged the development of Urmston, Flixton, Crumpsall and Prestwich. The historian John Stevenson provides an insight into the scale of commuter services when he states: 'the south Manchester suburbs of Heaton Mersey, Didsbury, Withington and Chorlton were linked by a frequent and rapid commuter service to Manchester Central by the 1880s, providing them with forty trains a day into the centre of Manchester, with an average frequency of ten minutes during peak periods'.[4] It has already been shown how stage coaches became more efficient and reduced journey times. By mid-century, the transport system was a mixture of a handful of inns still operating coaching and new omnibus services (a new form of horse-draw bus that could accommodate more passengers), and many termini where one could catch a particular service, such as Market Street and Oldham Street, on a par with modern-day bus stops.[5] The change in the way transport operated was a more progressive transition from the 1850s onwards as railways expanded their routes, coaching services gradually declined and inns become a less prominent part of the transport network. Omnibuses took over transportation within the immediate locality and these did not require inns as stopping points.[6] In 1852, a new style of omnibus was introduced which held many more passengers and cut operating costs, and by the 1860s newer vehicles could carry around 21 passengers inside with more on the top of the vehicle, and they were drawn by four horses. These operated a regular service around the city and within an 8-mile radius to other towns and villages.[7] About 1877 saw the emergence of tramcars that ran on rails, first powered by horses, then by electricity.[8] By 1886, most services for transporting people were now operating from street-based termini, and a modern transport system had effectively been born.

Manchester had several main railway stations that grew around the edge of the centre, and between 1830 and 1844 six key rail routes to the major cities of the country were in operation. By the second part of the century these had developed rapidly. The first station, as we have seen, was on Liverpool Road and opened in 1830 in line with the arrival of the railway line to Liverpool. The life of Liverpool Road Station was relatively short, since it was quickly superseded by Hunt's Bank (later Victoria) Station in 1844, which took over the services to Liverpool. Despite being closed to passengers, Liverpool Road Station became a central terminal for the movement of goods. Today, the site is the location of the fascinating Museum of Science and Industry and provides one of the best experiences one can have of the early railways, where the opulent booking hall and waiting room is now a silent reminder of its past glory and significance. Oxford Road Station is one of the smallest but busiest of Manchester's stations. Opened in 1849, it has traditionally covered destinations south and east of Manchester city centre. In 1857, the platforms were expanded to cope with the demand of passengers attending the Art Treasures Exhibition, such was the popularity of the event. In 1874, it was rebuilt and further improved to cope with the demand for rail travel. Manchester Piccadilly, Manchester's main train station, traces its heritage back to 1842, first as Store Street Station and subsequently London Road Station from 1847, and here the Manchester and Birmingham Railway Company operated. In 1849, a line connecting it to Oxford Road Station was opened and allowed some services to cut straight through the city centre. By the 1860s, London Road Station was so congested that in 1862 the station was completely rebuilt. Central Railway Station was opened in 1880. It was one of the main lines to St Pancras in London and was located next to the Midland Hotel, which was built to mirror the St Pancras end of the line. Central Station closed in 1969 and services were diverted to Oxford Road and Piccadilly Stations. The former Central Station is now the GMEX exhibition centre, and the remnants of the lines can be found in one of the most unusual car parks in the underground former goods yard.

It was not only road and rail services that had expanded. Manchester's water-based transport was transformed by the construction of the Manchester Ship Canal. Manchester's trading potential had always been somewhat curtailed and reliant on Liverpool which, as the nearest port to Manchester, had a monopoly on the transfer of raw materials and goods between Manchester and the rest of the world. However, trade was slower than it could be and it was decided to overcome this by turning Manchester into a port that was not reliant on Liverpool docks. The Ship Canal was designed to make Manchester more competitive than places such as Germany and the USA, which were catching up with Manchester's previous dominance on global trade. The Manchester Ship Canal was an engineering project like no other and was a risky undertaking, both financially and due to the engineering obstacles it faced. In 1882, a report detailing the case for a ship canal was published and, as one would expect, the project was not universally welcomed, since the railway companies, the Bridgewater Canal and the Port of Liverpool would all be detrimentally affected by such an undertaking and faced unwanted financial competition. There were problems getting the proposal for the new canal through Parliament, largely because of vocal opposition from the Mersey Docks and Harbour Board and the Liverpool Chamber of Commerce. The relentless arguments resulted in the costs of the project rising quite remarkably even before construction had begun. It took three attempts at putting the legislation through Parliament, in part because of support from Salford and Warrington Councils who provided strong backing for the project and did not give up in their attempts to see it through. Finally, it successfully passed through Parliament in 1885, though Liverpool authorities were still vehemently opposed, and in fact concessions were made to appease the opposition on Merseyside, which included rerouting the canal by an extra 15 miles. It was 1887 before there were sufficient funds and the problems were resolved to allow construction to begin. Even when work did begin it faced some difficult situations. First, a contractor died in 1889, casting a shadow over an already difficult project. Soon after, in 1890, floods damaged some of the construction work. Finally, by 1891 it was clear there was not enough capital to complete the project and Manchester's authorities agreed to subsidise the work

42 Construction of the Manchester Ship Canal, Latchford Lock. (Copyright University of Manchester)

to the tune of £3 million. The canal finally opened on 1 January 1894, with a royal official opening on 21 May 1894 by Queen Victoria, well over budget but an engineering triumph. Trade began slowly and there were further concerns that it would not live up to its promises, and critics of the canal were carefully watching with interest, likely hoping it would fail. However, trade began to flourish, and, as predicted, it badly affected Liverpool's income as a port, and the 35 miles of waterway and complex navigation systems turned Manchester into an inland port, ending the dependence on Liverpool.[9]

From Industry to Culture

By the mid-nineteenth century, Manchester was the workshop of the world and the epicentre of trade and industry. However, following on from other exhibitions, those at the heart of Manchester's commerce and civic society wanted to show a more cultural and artistic side to life in the city. Displays of the nation's artistic and commercial talents were showcased at a number of high-profile events exhibiting an array of art, culture and scientific innovation. Displays of artistic genius were inspired by other illustrious exhibitions, such as London's

Great Exhibition of 1851, and Dublin in 1853. In 1857, Manchester held an exhibition that was a demonstration of its Victorian success and position in the world of trade, industry and, importantly, high culture. In fact, Manchester was the last place that an exhibition of this kind was expected to take place and it certainly caused some ripples of interest, particularly from the south where London was seen as the cultural centre of the country, not the industrious north. For example, the *Illustrated London News* commented:

> The new-made city hurls back upon her detractors the charge that she is too deeply absorbed in the pursuit of material wealth to devote her energies to the finer arts. True it is that the staple industries of the city have but little kindred with the beautiful in art, and that labour is the lot of Manchester.[10]

The motivation for the exhibition came from John Deane, a cotton manufacturer, and Sir Thomas Fairbairn, son of the famous William Fairbairn, who followed in the family engineering business. Fairbairn was well embedded in Mancunian society, being a member of the Literary and Philosophical Society and attending Cross Street Chapel. The intention was to request that holders of major art collections open them up for the all the public to see, regardless of class, and one can imagine a working-class person seeing such wonders for the first time. Most collectors were amenable to the request and subscriptions were quickly raised and, following a meeting at Manchester Town Hall, over £72,000 was raised from local merchants in a display of not only industrial wealth but civic pride in Manchester. The monarchy was keen on the idea, in particular Prince Albert, who had endorsed the Great Exhibition of 1851 in London. The Art Treasures Exhibition, as it became known, was located at nearby Old Trafford, beginning on 5 May and lasting until 17 October of the same year – there were over 16,000 paintings, and well over a million visitors passed through its doors. Dignitaries included high-class society from across Europe and famous British Victorians such as politicians Benjamin Disraeli and William Gladstone, the poet Lord Tennyson, and novelists Elizabeth Gaskell and Charles Dickens.[11] The arts on offer ranged from Michelangelo to Constable, Holbein to Raphael to Turner. It was simply the largest artist collection ever seen in one place, certainly in the United Kingdom if not the world. Special trains at reduced rates were laid on to convey visitors from all over the country, and as we have seen, the platform at Oxford Road Station was expanded to accommodate visitors travelling there. For a place that had demonstrated industrial prowess, it also showed a cultural and artistic side of Manchester as a global powerhouse.[12] Even the Hallé Orchestra grew out of Charles Hallé's involvement with the Art Treasures Exhibition when he was asked to put together a small orchestra to play for Prince Albert at the opening ceremony. Hallé duly obliged and decided he liked the idea so much that he kept his band of musicians together, forming the fledgling orchestra. Even Queen Victoria made an appearance, attending on 30 June. So the industrial city had become a cultural city.[13]

Towards the latter part of the nineteenth century, one of the finest libraries was created. It is another example of Manchester's wealth and status being flaunted in a cultural context. The John Rylands Library, which is now part of the University of Manchester, is one of the best libraries in the world, not only for its bibliographic contents but for the building which houses it treasures. John Rylands was Manchester's first multimillionaire, having been successful in the family's textile company. By the mid-1850s, he was rich enough to move to Longford Hall in Stretford, where he began accumulating a library of books. It was Enriqueta Rylands who had the original idea to build a library in tribute to her husband. After John died in 1888, the library building was embarked upon. Its Gothic style is attributed to its architect Basil Champneys and it is often regarded as his finest piece of work. It took ten years to build at a cost of around half a million pounds. The main reading room is the focal point for the library, with a statue of John and Enriqueta at each end.

Manchester was noted for its warehouses and by the mid-nineteenth century many that looked more like palaces than commercial buildings were being built. Many were adopting an Italian 'Palazzo' style, inspired by the architecture of places such as fourteenth-century Florence and Venice, and the idea behind

43 John Rylands
Library. (Courtesy
of Google Maps)

44 Former Watt's Warehouse, currently the Britannia Hotel on Portland Street.

it was to create a sense of an industrial renaissance just as there had been an Italian early modern artistic renaissance. These new palazzo warehouses were the Victorians displaying their commercial prowess. Watt's Warehouse, on Portland Street, is now the Britannia Hotel.[14]

Manchester's educational institutions were also developing, and here we see the Victoria University of Manchester emerging out of Owens College, which was founded in 1851, and from 1872 it incorporated the Royal School of Medicine and Surgery, which had been formed in 1824 as a medical school. Owens College was created by a legacy of £96,942 left in 1846 by the wealthy industrialist John Owens to establish a college for education on non-sectarian lines. It opened in 1851 in a house on Quay Street. Its first few years were diffi-cult; the only English precedent for a modern university college was in London, and most Manchester merchants saw little value in the education on offer, pre-ferring that their sons join family businesses as soon as possible. However, from the 1860s, the college created a new vision, and its leading professors looked to German universities that emphasised the creation and not just the transmis-sion of knowledge. For them, research was the key ingredient of a university; it advanced knowledge and was a potential source of material benefits. It also gave students the experience of facing the unknown and problem solving. This became a feature of both an education in the humanities as well as the sciences, and a college education finally came to be valued as the key preparation for a professional career. By 1870, the college had grown to the point that it needed new premises and building started on the current Oxford Road site. The first building, that of the John Owens building, was completed in 1873. The group of buildings that make up the Old Quadrangle of the university were finished in 1903 and designed by notable architect Alfred Waterhouse, who also designed Manchester Town Hall. The new university buildings included the first galleries of the Manchester Museum, whose natural history collection had been amassed by a local society and went from strength to strength. From 1873, a large chemistry laboratory on Burlington Street and a new medical school on Coupland Street were constructed. Clinical teaching was provided at the Manchester Royal Infirmary, which remained in Piccadilly until 1908 but later moved to Oxford Road, just south of the university. In 1880, Owens College became the first constituent part of the federal Victoria University, England's first civic university, which later included colleges in Liverpool and Leeds.

National and Local Politics

The Free Trade Hall was symbolic of Manchester's Liberal political tradition of the nineteenth century, where middle-class politicians such as Richard Cobden led the Anti-Corn Law League which, as we saw in the last chapter, worked to repeal the corn laws that artificially raised the price of food, and campaigned for free trade. The group that advocated such policies became known as the Manchester School, which adopted the theories of Adam Smith and advocated economic liberalist policies, shaping government policy on these matters. The hall itself was funded by public subscription and completed in 1856. In 1858, it became the home of the Hallé Orchestra, which remained there until they relocated to their new home, the Bridgewater Hall, in 1996. The hall is built on the site of the Peterloo Massacre, and Figure 45 includes the red plaque to remind us of the history of the site.

Whilst politics during the second part of the nineteenth century was much quieter than the turbulence of the earlier period, the desire for further political reforms was as strong as ever. It was at this time that two movements emerge that would push for progressive political reforms, and Manchester was at the

45 The Free Trade Hall.

heart of both. The first was dominated by the rise of a new socialist political movement that would eventually lead to the Labour Party. The second was the rise of women's campaigns for the right to vote. The Great Reform Act of 1832 was criticised for not going far enough in extending the vote to working-class men. However, women were not even part of this process. The Second Reform Act of 1867 did extend the right to vote to include some rent payers as well as owners, and removed other conditions that affected the democratic rights of men, and in Manchester the Second Reform Act had the effect of doubling the electorate.[15] This went even further in 1884 when the franchise was opened up to include all male house owners.[16] So these pieces of legislation created a mass of politically aware but inexperienced voters who were about to influence politics, both locally and nationally. Also, there were only two parties to choose from, the Conservatives and Liberals, and neither offered what this new electorate of working-class voters wanted. Consequently, Manchester, as a socialist and working-class centre, was at the forefront of a new progressive political thinking that led to the emergence of a formalised socialist party that would represent this new body of working-class voters. This came in the form of the

Social Democratic Federation (SDF), which was founded in the city during the mid-1880s. It began as a small but active group and their campaigns eventually fed into the work of the newly created Independent Labour Party (ILP) that emerged around 1892. The SDF lost momentum mainly because of their slightly overzealous revolutionary ambition, possibly with the exception of their campaigns on unemployment, which proved more effective. The ILP endorsed a similar socialist manifesto in line with the working-class of Manchester but their remit was much wider and less revolutionary than that of the SDF. It was not just about conveying a socialist message to the masses but the creation of proper socialist representation in Parliament now that the franchise had been opened up more widely, and ensuring that these new voters had a party they felt represented their needs. The most powerful figure in expressing this was Robert Blatchford, who vented his views via his weekly newspaper, the *Clarion*. Blatchford was Manchester's first ILP branch president and his socialist principles opposed any association with industrial capitalism. He also conveyed these views in his work *Merrie England*, which adopted a more holistic and community approach to politics by encouraging cycling, signing, rambling and other such social activities. He made the socialist movement distinct from both the Liberals and Tories, both of whom he saw as enemies of the working-class man.[17] It was Keir Hardie who then took up the leadership of the ILP at national level.

For men, political rights were taking shape slowly but surely, but women were increasingly being left behind. The franchise had indeed been expanded, which the early radicals and Chartists had so long campaigned for, but it was male suffrage they achieved; female franchise was some way off. Whilst the 1867 Reform Bill had extended male voting rights, it was a disappointment to women whose expectations were failed miserably. It was here that marked the arrival of the Women's Suffrage Movement, and Manchester, as a political hotspot, became the location for the emergence of women's campaigns for the franchise. Lydia Becker became the secretary of the Manchester National Society for Women's Suffrage in the late 1860s and she was instrumental in promoting the organisation. The women's movement at this time operated a respectable, and some would argue modest campaign, in mustering support, particularly amongst middle-class educated women who had time on their hands to devote their energies to the cause. Lydia was born in 1827 in Cooper Street, Manchester and was the eldest of fifteen children. She became involved in the Women's Suffrage Movement after the politician John Stuart Mill petitioned Parliament on the issue. Unlike her parents, she adopted Liberal views and made friendships with reformers such as Jacob Bright and Dr Richard Pankhurst. After Lydia's death in 1890, the political activist Millicent Fawcett took the mantle. However, their voice was increasingly crowded out and some in the movement felt they needed stronger tactics. These came in the form of Emmeline Pankhurst, who from an early age realised what it was like to be a woman in a man's world. Born in 1858, in Moss Side, Pankhurst was introduced to the campaign for women's rights at the tender age of just 14. She eventually married the lawyer and politician, Dr Richard Pankhurst, who had long supported the women's campaign and Lydia Becker's work. They went on to have five children, of which two, Christabel and Sylvia, would go on to campaign with their mother. Emmeline supported the Women's Franchise League, and when this ceased she attempted to join the ILP, in part because of her friendship with Labour leader Keir Hardie, but was initially refused membership simply because she was a woman. However, by the turn of the twentieth century little progress had been made and their campaigning became more militant in nature. This story continues as we head toward the Edwardian era in the next chapter.

Civic Pride

Manchester lost its manorial form of government in 1838 when the town was incorporated. In 1853, it became a city and out of this emerged a new civic pride which was reflected in the buildings that appeared, and in the attempts to improve the quality of life for all its citizens. Administratively, Manchester was governed from the town hall, the original building of which was located in King Street. This had been constructed during the 1820s and housed a number of departments, including committee rooms, the Chief Constable's office, a surveyor's office, and the Treasurer's department. However, this soon outgrew its usefulness and lacked the impact that a major city like Manchester should have. The Victorian town hall was not just a practical administrative centre but also a statement of civic pride. Plans to replace the town hall commenced in 1863 and these were both practical and conveyed Victorian opulence worthy of a cosmopolitan global city. After deliberations, the Albert Square location was chosen as the new town hall site. Alfred Waterhouse was appointed as the architect and the foundation stone was laid on 26 October 1868. The new town hall was opened by the Mayor of the time, Abel Heywood, in 1877.

46 Manchester Town Hall.

47 The Albert Memorial, Albert Square.

The architecture said much about Manchester's industrial greatness and place in the world. The decoration was adorned with cotton flowers to represent the cotton industry and bees as a symbol of hard work. As has been shown in previous chapters, the Great Hall is surrounded by *Manchester Murals* by Ford Madox Brown, which illustrate some of the key moments in Manchester's history, from the Roman occupation to industrial prowess. The town hall is fronted by Albert Square, incorporating the Albert memorial statue to reflect Prince Albert's role in the Art Treasures Exhibition.

Manchester was quickly developing a consumer culture towards the end of the nineteenth century that can still be felt in the city today. Here, a number of large flagship department stores opened, such as Lewis's and Kendal Milne. Lewis's was located at the top of Market Street and was largely aimed at the aspirations of a better paid working and lower-middle classes. The company began in Liverpool in the 1850s and opened its next store in Manchester in 1877. Its facilities even included a ballroom on the fifth floor. It remained in business right up until 2002 when clothing retailer Primark took over the premises. A more affluent department store, however, could be seen in Kendal Milne's. Kendal's origins can be traced back to 1796 when John Watts opened a drapery near Deansgate, and in 1832 this moved to different premises further along Deansgate. In 1836, the store was sold by the Watts to three employees and it became Kendal, Milne & Faulkner. Faulkner died in 1862 and the company became Kendal Milne & Co. and it then began expanding into furniture and upholstery. By 1884, Thomas Kendal retired and the daily operations were managed by John Dewhurst Milne and sons of Thomas Kendal. By the 1890s, it had opened a number of departments and a tea room. The store went from strength to strength, catering for Manchester's wealthier clients. Today it is run by the House of Fraser group and is still a flagship store that dominates Deansgate and still bears the Kendals' name. Another consumer experience was that of Barton Arcade, between Deansgate and St Ann's Square, and is one of the best examples of its time. Today it is a hidden gem that can still be enjoyed, but at the time of opening in 1871 it was sheer Victorian opulence of iron and glass which lent a conservatory feel to the shopping experience.[18]

At the other end of the consumer experience was the Co-operative movement that found its administrative home in central Manchester, at No. 1 Balloon Street. Originating in Rochdale in 1844, the 'Pioneers' developed a system where profits were shared amongst its members, which was affectionately known as the 'divi', and they provided cheaper goods for those that could not afford very much, particularly basic food stuffs. The Co-op split into a number of different parts, with the Co-operative Wholesale Society, or CWS, in 1863 and the Co-operative Insurance Company in 1867. In 1863 the Co-operative Wholesale and Industrial Provident Society Ltd was created in Manchester by a number of local co-operatives in the Lancashire and Yorkshire areas. By 1872, this had grown rapidly, servicing Co-op stores across the country. By 1900, there were almost 1,500 co-operative societies registered around the country and two million members. The area around Balloon Street and Dantzig Street has become a famous address for the society's headquarters address and the centre of the wholesale part of the business. The site housed a warehouse for the grocery part of the business which was acquired in 1869. The Co-op was mainly based in smaller grocery stores in towns around Manchester, but its central offices can still be seen here today, with the notable CIS building and New Century House recently joined by a new flagship building close to the original Balloon Street complex.[19]

Conclusion

The stability of the mid-Victorian years came in the form of displays of culture and industry that were statements of Manchester's place in the world and developments in politics. The Art Treasures Exhibition was on a scale not seen certainly in the region if not the country at the time, and it was a clear demonstration to place Manchester as not just a place of trade and industry but one of art and culture. Manchester's elevation to city status reinforced this, and new buildings reflected a new sense of civic pride and status. Whilst on the surface politics appeared calmer, there were continued campaigns for equality, and this time they came from women, who were excluded from any political voice, and middle-class educated women were taking up the cause. As we head towards the dawn of a new century, the conflicts between women and the establishment began to take on a new militancy and it is here that the story turns next.

Notes

1 *Manchester Courier*, 2 April 1853.
2 Best, G., *Mid-Victorian Britain 1851–1875* (Fontana Press, 1985), p. 29.

3 Gunn, S., *The Public Culture of the Victorian Middle Class: ritual and authority in the English industrial city, 1840–1914* (Manchester University Press, 2007), p. 46.

4 Stevenson, J., *British Society 1914 to 1945* (Pelican, 1984), p. 25.

5 *Slater's Trade Directory for Manchester and Salford* (1841); *Whellan's Directory for Manchester and Salford* (1852).

6 Manchester Corporation, *A Hundred Years*, p. 15.

7 Baines, *History, Directory and Gazetteer,* p. 391.

8 Manchester Corporation, *A Hundred Years*, pp. 6–7.

9 Kidd, *Manchester*, p. 115.

10 Pergam E., *The Manchester Art Treasures Exhibition of 1857: entrepreneurs, connoisseurs and the public* (Ashgate, 2011), p. 14.

11 http://www.victorianweb.org/victorian/art/institutions/manchester1857.html [accessed 28 December 2016].

12 Hunt, T., *Building Jersualem: the rise and fall of the Victorian city* (Phoenix Press, 2005), pp. 189–91.

13 Hunt, *Building Jerusalem*, pp. 221–6.

14 Gunn, *The Public Culture*, p. 40.

15 Walton, J., *Lancashire: a social history* (Manchester University Press, 1987), p. 258.

16 Hanham, *Elections and Party Management* (Longmans, 1959), p. ix.

17 Hill, J., 'Manchester and Salford Politics and the Early Development of the Independent Labour Party', *International Journal of Social History*, 26(2), (1981).

18 houseoffraserarchive.co.uk

19 Kidd, *Manchester*, p. 108.

eight

EDWARDIAN MANCHESTER

Manchester is a city which has witnessed a great many stirring episodes, especially of a
political character. Generally speaking, its citizens have been liberal in their sentiments,
defenders of free speech and liberty of opinion.

Emmeline Pankhurst (1914)

Introduction

In 1901, Queen Victoria died and the new Edwardian era began with the
reign of Edward VII, to coincide with the new century. This chapter looks at
Manchester from the turn of the twentieth century through to the 1930s, a
period very much marked by both continuity and change in Mancunian society.
Continuity came in the form of working-class and women's political campaigns.
The relentless pressure from women's political organisations, namely the suffragettes, ultimately led to success, but their struggle was often physical and
brutal. Life and culture had become both cosmopolitan and consumerist. Yet
society was changing in the sense that the industries that made Manchester
such a global leader were losing their momentum, as the cotton industry that
had been so great was in terminal decline, and the economy of Manchester
had to adjust to new circumstances. A different form of urban development
emerges as Manchester Corporation invested in housing and local services to
offset the potential economic decline and create employment. This resulted in
districts on the edge of the city centre becoming key residential areas as new
mass housing estates become located on the periphery of the city. The onset of

the First World War in 1914 made most places change quite sharply because of the loss of life that badly affected most communities in the country, and Manchester was no exception. Manchester was part of the effort to send Pals regiments to the front line, and no sooner was this war over than another one loomed on the horizon. This chapter takes the story to the eve of the Second World War in 1939.

Politics and the Women's Suffrage Campaign

By the early part of the twentieth century, Manchester had one of the most organised and effective labour movements in the country and was reminiscent of Manchester as the centre of radical politics of the early nineteenth century, something that had almost disappeared in a sea of mid-nineteenth-century Victorian stability. Manchester was the place where some key notable local women had great significance in national politics, in particular through social-ist and women's causes. The last chapter introduced the Pankhurst family, with Emmeline, husband Richard, and daughters Christabel and Sylvia. There was also Ellen Wilkinson who managed to secure representation in Parliament as one of the first women MPs. It was in 1903 that the Pankhurst family officially came onto the political scene, when Emmeline and Christabel helped to form the Women's Social and Political Union (WSPU). Emmeline Goulden was born on 15 July 1858 in Sloan Street, Moss Side and was the eldest of ten siblings. She was politically aware at a young age, particularly when it came to school-ing, and she witnessed how her brother's education was taken far more seriously than her own. Emmeline went to a girls' school but this merely taught how to run a good home. In her biography she recalls this troubling issue of inequality:

> It was a custom of my father and mother to make the round of our bedrooms every night before going themselves to bed. When they entered my room that night I was still awake, but for some reason I chose to feign slumber. My father bent over me, shielding the candle flame with his big hand. I cannot know exactly what thought was in his mind as he gazed down at me, but I heard him say, somewhat sadly, 'what a pity she wasn't born a lad'.[1]

Emmeline was 14 when she went to her first suffrage meeting, where she was inspired by Lydia Becker who was then secretary to the Manchester Suffrage

Committee. One of the founders of the suffrage movement in Manchester was Dr Richard Pankhurst, to whom she eventually married in 1879. Christabel was her first child, soon followed by Sylvia, then two more children followed. Her fifth child was born in 1890. Motherhood did not hinder her tireless campaigns for women's equality and she ended up on the executive board of the Women's Suffrage Association. In 1898, Richard died, a devastating blow to their nineteen years of happy marriage, and led her to taking a salaried role as a registrar for births and deaths.

In 1900, Keir Hardie was returned to Parliament as Labour MP for Merthyr Tydfil and this marked a hopeful turning point in the suffragette campaign as the Labour Party was in favour of political rights for women, and especially so due to the Pankhurst family connections with the ILP.[2] In October 1903, at Nelson Street the Women's Social and Political Union (WSPU) was born. The WSPU was an all-women suffrage organisation that focused more on action than words, and some would argue too much action, but having seen the lack of progress thus far, the Pankhursts and the WSPU had to consider other strategies that were open to them. Oldham mill girl Annie Kenney, along with an increasingly large female following, became known for their physical and direct action that often led to injury, damage to property and arrest. Most notably, they engaged in hunger strikes and were often force fed in prison, which led to the passing of the Cat and Mouse Act in 1913 where prisoners that were ill from hunger strikes were released, only to be rearrested again once they had recovered, thus starting the force feeding once more. Emmeline, Annie and Christabel received regular prison sentences, where they often staged hunger strikes, and were force fed.

48 The Pankhurst house on Nelson Street.

49 Emmeline, Christabel and Sylvia Pankhurst. (Courtesy of Manchester Libraries, Information and Archives, Manchester City Council)

Christabel eventually took leadership of the WSPU, as the group became increasingly antagonistic towards the government and vice versa. In 1905, Christabel and Annie attained wide publicity for their campaign when they interrupted a meeting of the Liberal Party at the Free Trade Hall. Christabel questioned Winston Churchill, who was speaking at the event: 'If the Liberals were elected would they give women the vote?' After repeating the question and demanding an answer which they were never likely to receive, they were ejected from the meeting, and finally arrested when Christabel spat at a policeman. After refusing to pay the resulting fine, they were sent to prison for their actions, but this only served to widen the publicity for their cause, which was their ultimate aim.[3] It was in 1914 that the suffragettes finally halted their campaign, not because of the endless arrests but because of the onset of the First World War, and it was ironic that the women who opposed the establishment so vehemently stood side by side with the government to support the war effort. Women across the country became an intrinsic part of the war machine at home as men were conscripted to the front line. Was it the war effort that convinced Parliament to extend voting rights to all men over the age of 21 and to women over the age of 30, by passing the Representation of the People Act in 1918, or was it the fear of the suffrage campaign continuing as war had ended? This has been debated ever since, but the war did mark a turning point in women's political fortunes, and the franchise for women was extended in 1928 to all women over 21. It is ironic that Emmeline died just two weeks before this was passed, just missing out on seeing her hard work bear fruit.

Another notable local woman engaged in politics was Ellen Wilkinson, who was born in Chorlton-on-Medlock in 1891 to a fairly poor family. In 1910, Ellen joined the University of Manchester after winning a scholarship to study there. Here, she developed a keen interest in socialism, in particular the Fabian Society. She was also active in women's politics and social causes and eventually working for the National Union of Women's Suffrage Societies. During the First World War she was active in women's interests, supporting working women in wartime industries. She eventually went into mainstream politics, first in a trade union role and then later she entered Parliament in 1924 as MP for Middlesbrough East, and in 1935 MP for Jarrow. Around the time of the Second World War she became first a junior minister then Minister for Education.

Industrial Change

It is without doubt that the cotton industry peaked in 1913, just before the outbreak of the First World War. At this time, around 65 per cent of the world's cotton textiles were made in the region, but it was facing competition from countries as never before as they now had access to more modern machinery and a ready market. Manchester had always been heavily reliant on the Indian textiles market, which by the early twentieth century had become proficient at producing its own cloth. As the First World War struck, it marked the start of the end for King Cotton. By the 1920s, the cotton industry in Manchester had all but collapsed and the city was faced with the need to adapt its economy and develop post-war attempts at regeneration. High levels of unemployment and poverty were prevalent in areas that had already been poor, even at the height of the cotton industry's success, such as Miles Platting, Chorlton-on-Medlock, Hulme, Ancoats and Angel Meadow. Housing guru Sir Ernest Simon described Angel Meadow at this time:

No. 4 F Street. The general appearance and condition of this house inside are very miserable. It is a dark house and the plaster on the passage walls, in particular, was in a bad condition. There is no sink or tap in the house; they are in the small yard, consequently in the frosty weather the family is without water. In this house live a man and wife and seven children ranging from 15 to 1, and a large, if varying, number of rats.[4]

So, when the cotton industry began to decline these areas were particularly affected. It was left to local authorities, businessmen and other stakeholders to offer a programme of regeneration and provide new business and employment opportunities that would replace the dying industries and also provide longer-term sustainable solutions. It was at this time that a diversification in Manchester's economic base took place, and the development of the industrial Trafford Park was in response to Manchester's economic woes. Some 3 miles outside Manchester, Trafford Park emerged as a productive area for engineering, particularly during the wartime periods where the area became noted for aircraft, munitions and other vital industries for the war effort. It housed key engineering plants such as Rolls Royce, Vickers, James Gresham Engineers and W.T. Glovers electrical engineering. Even food manufacturers such as Brooke Bond and Kellogg's were located there. So here was an area that helped to stave off the mass economic depression of the 1930s with employment opportunities for the south Lancashire area which was not as badly affected as other areas of the country in terms of economic depression and unemployment. Henry Ford initially set up his first European vehicle plant here, where 6,000 Model Ts were produced by 1913. However, they eventually moved to Dagenham in the early 1930s.[5]

One of the more famous engineering plants was that of A.V. Roe whose influence was to become significant as Europe headed towards war. A.V. Roe was at the forefront of aircraft production, a new industry that would lead to a new world of aviation technology. It all began with Alliot Verdon Roe, who was born in 1877 in nearby Patricroft. He actually began his career in the rail industry at the Lancashire and Yorkshire Railway near Horwich, but his engineering skills extended to marine and motor engineering. However, it was aircraft that he became renowned for, and he faced little competition, as it was an industry in its infancy. He had already began developing a name for himself through dabbling with aircraft at Brooklands and Lee Marshes, where he finally achieved his first controlled successful flight in July 1909, and this led to the financial backing of his brother who owned the Everard Webbing factory at Brownsfield Mill in Great Ancoats Street. Here the 'Avro' name was born and the company took off. It employed around 34 people, producing a triplane and a tractor biplane. They also rented a shed at Brooklands Flying Grounds where their aircraft was sold. The company developed fast, becoming a limited company in 1913. It was no wonder that Avro's order books were so full at the onset of the First World War, and expansion on an unprecedented scale took place, since the war led to a number of military contracts for aircraft, and this expansion in production led to the Brownsfield Mill site no longer being adequate. In 1913, some of their operation moved to Miles Platting, utilising some former railways wagon sheds, when Groves Brewers helped to finance their move. They improved upon their aircraft design and the government were so impressed with their Avro 504 model that they began placing orders. Eventually Brownsfield Mill became surplus to requirements and they let it go.[6] However, it was not long before they also outgrew the Miles Platting site, and the Avro 504 was produced in the extension to Mather and Platt's Engineers in nearby Newton Heath. Such was their growth that by 1919 even this site was fully operational at maximum capacity. The Avro 504 was especially popular with the Royal Flying Corps and the Royal Naval Air Service, and around 9,000 aircraft were produced. The scale of production resulted in a further site near Portsmouth being opened. One would have thought that the end of the war would have affected the company's potential for survival, but they quickly adapted to form a transport company, located at Alexandra Park Aerodrome near Didsbury, offering flights to Blackpool. By 1924, this operation had moved to Woodford in Cheshire,

50 Avro Manchester Mark 1. (Copyright Imperial War Museum)

though production still remained at Newton Heath, where assembly took place, and Woodford became a testing ground.

It was not long before war struck again and, as problems grew in Europe in the period leading up to 1939, Avro developed a further site at Greengate, close to Middleton. Here, the famous Lancaster bomber was built. By this time, Ringway Airport had opened (which is now Manchester International) for use by the RAF, where an experimental department was also opened up. A further production site at Yeadon Aerodrome was also opened (today's Leeds Bradford Airport) where a number of key aircraft models went into production.[7]

Manchester and the First World War

In 1914, war broke out, and whilst it did not directly come to our shores, our soldiers were at the forefront of the fighting in Europe. Many towns and cities sent 'Pals' battalions, groups of men from their own localities who formed key parts of the British Army, the intention being to extend the comradeship that already existed amongst communities and occupations. This sense of home was badly needed to get them through the ordeal, assuming they would indeed survive, which a great many did not. Many were from the same trade and recruited in cities of the north such as Manchester. The Manchester Pals were organised into eight battalions and formed part of the older Manchester Regiment which had been in existence since the 1790s. The First World War was a conflict that relied on volunteers signing up and such was the determination for many to volunteer that in Manchester a crowd stormed the town hall to demand a quicker processing of recruits. In all, the city managed to raise fifteen battalions and up to 20,000 men volunteering in the first month of the war.[8] Between September 1914 and the spring of 1915, Heaton Park, Manchester's largest public park, became a large military camp for the Pals battalions and it was here that volunteers were trained as soldiers, and unfortunately many left to face the Somme.[9] One of the largest contingent of Pals in the country were recruited in Manchester battalions, and which included the 16th and 17th and the 18th Clerks and Warehousemen's battalions. They say that war is a great leveller of social class, and this was clearly felt in a city whose member of the Pals ranged from factory workers to businessmen. Many were clerks and warehouse staff, others were merchants and business owners. The casualties were heavy, with around 13,000 lost in the Manchester Regiment.[10]

Urban Development

During the Edwardian era, urban development in Manchester was twofold. First, the city was increasing in size as outer districts and suburbs were being swallowed up in its urban sprawl. Second, there was development of the city centre as part of an aspiration to create a modern city that was moving away from its Victorian past. In terms of Manchester's overall increase in size, it had begun to develop as an urban area from the 1838 incorporation, when some outer districts were subsumed by central Manchester. In 1838, central Manchester was joined by Chorlton-on-Medlock, Hulme, Ardwick, Beswick and Cheetham. It took some time for the next round of districts to join, but in 1885 Harpurhey, Bradford and Rusholme became part of Manchester. Between 1890 and 1913, many more outer suburbs became part of Manchester's urban sprawl, including Blackley, Moston, Crumpsall, Newton Heath, Openshaw, Kirkmanshulme, West Gorton, Heaton Park, Moss Side, Withington, Burnage, Chorlton-cum-Hardy, Didsbury, Gorton and Levenshulme. There was a hiatus until 1931 when Wythenshawe joined Manchester.[11]

Investment in central Manchester was turning Cottonopolis into a modern twentieth-century city, but regeneration was also badly needed to prevent post-war economic decay, and Manchester Corporation had to act to prevent a decline in the city and region. The great housing pioneer of his time, Sir Ernest Simon, stated that:

> In Manchester practically all the houses in the slum belt, numbering about 80,000, will have to be demolished and replaced by modern houses of flats, before the city's housing can be regarded as satisfactory. This means that there will be splendid opportunity for re-planning the central area on the best modern lines and for making a comprehensive plan for Manchester's whole future development; it is most important that this opportunity should be utilised to the full, so that all the congestion and ill-health and waste caused by the lack of any planning when the slum belt was first built may be prevented in the future. The essential thing is that all the work which is done – clearance, rebuilding and new development – should be carried out as a part of a unified scheme; experts are unanimous in condemning a policy of piecemeal slum clearance without regard to their relationship to the requirements of the city as a whole.[12]

Land was purchased to develop large council housing estates, the main one of which was in Wythenshawe, which was designed to boost the local economy by providing jobs and to give residents the latest in new housing and estate design. In 1926, land near Wythenshawe Hall was purchased to provide this major new housing estate, and it was well ahead of its time in design and purpose, offering houses, open green spaces, shops and other communal facilities. Some have argued that it was also a means of preventing unemployment and potential social unrest.[13] Wythenshawe became the UK's first municipally owned satellite town and by 1933 there were almost 22,000 new council houses in Manchester's suburbs, and Wythenshawe itself contained around 40,000 residents. Wythenshawe was the vision of Sir Ernest Simon, and his intention was to plan a garden suburb to house 100,000 people. By 1939, 8,000 houses had been built here and the housing offered a standard of comfort far higher than had been possible in the past.[14] Manchester Corporation were by now on a programme of slum clearance in the city centre, and this had the effect of taking people further out into Manchester's fringes, with fewer people living in the centre. This allowed more businesses and consumerism to flourish in the centre instead, and created a division where cities were places where people worked and shopped but did not live.[15] However, such was the demand for housing in the city that even by the 1930s there was still a housing shortage, and in Manchester 49,000 people were still living in what were regarded as nineteenth-century standards.[16]

Manchester Corporation's redevelopment of the city centre, in many respects, turned its back on its traditional Victorian architecture and heritage. The desire to create a new cosmopolitan city meant out with the old and in with the new and there was little interest in preserving the past for future generations. It was as if Manchester was embarrassed about being the former workshop of the world, and instead a rash of new art-deco-style buildings began to appear in the centre. However, many fine Victorian buildings remained and the newer ones, in fact, blended well with the older buildings that still existed, such as the Manchester Exchange, town hall and John Rylands Library. In the 1930s, the town hall was extended, to include a new council chamber, gas and electricity departments and a rates hall for people to pay their bills. Manchester Central Library was built in what became a civic centre, where key transport routes passed through to showcase Manchester's newfound pride. Manchester Central Library was (and still is) a marvel of Manchester's inter-war architecture. Costing in the region of £600,000, it was one of the largest library reading rooms after the British Library in London, accommodating 300 people and housing around 1 million books. We have seen how, in 1852, the first public

51 Front of Manchester Central Library, St Peter's Square.

52 Rear of Manchester Central Library, St Peter's Square.

free library was established at Campfield. This site eventually became insufficient for its needs and was relocated to the former town hall in King Street. It subsequently moved again, this time to a section of the Infirmary in Piccadilly in 1912. The idea to build a new library had been in the background for some time but the First World War postponed any hope of taking the plans further. However, the idea returned in 1919 when this was discussed alongside the construction of a town hall extension which was completed in 1926. The architects' competition was won by E. Vincent Harris, and the new library housed an exhibition hall, theatre, research rooms and lecture rooms.[17] Its circular design reflected the style of architecture seen in American buildings of the time, yet it also had resonances with Roman architecture, having a similar appearance to the ancient Pantheon. It was on 17 July 1934 that the current central library was opened by King George V. Other key new buildings of the Edwardian era included the Ship Canal building, which was constructed in 1926 and typified this new style of building that was taller than previous buildings and symbolic of redevelopment in its vicinity. Sunlight House on Quay Street was built in 1932 and at the time was the city's tallest commercial building. Edward Lutyen's Midland Bank on King Street was complete in 1935 and Kendal Milne's department store in 1938.

53 Kendal's, formerly Kendal Milne on Deansgate.

It was not just civic buildings that were emerging as architectural marvels. Manchester's Midland Hotel is one of the finest hotels ever built in the region. It was opened in 1903 and at the time was located next to Manchester's Central Railway station and built by the Midland Railway to reflect a style of architecture that mirrored the opposite end of the line at St Pancras Hotel and station in London. It is ironic that a building of this scale and opulence should be built so close to the site of the Peterloo Massacre. Even today, the Midland Hotel is one of the most iconic buildings in Manchester, hosting a range of important and high-profile events, and notable for the political party conference season. Its location, on the edge of St Peter's Square overlooking the Central Library, reinforced the new modernity that was taking shape in the city centre. It was at the Midland Hotel in 1904 that a meeting between Charles Stewart and Frederick Henry Joyce led to the formation of the famous Rolls-Royce Company.

Another of Manchester's distinctive hotels is the Palace Hotel at the top of Oxford Road, which has provided a distinctive part of the skyline for about 130 years. It was the former Refuge Assurance Building and is a statement of Victorian opulence architecture in terracotta with a notable clock tower. It was designed by Alfred Waterhouse at the end of the nineteenth century and is now a Grade II listed building. The Refuge Assurance Company began in 1895 and the building was its head office and a local landmark. In 1989, the Refuge Assurance closed, and it was converted into a hotel in 1994, and is now one of Manchester's top places to stay.

54 The Midland Hotel.

55 The former Refuge Assurance Building, later the Palace Hotel.

Intellectual Manchester

Manchester's key intellectual institutions were at the cutting edge of art and science. The University of Manchester had acquired its charter as a university by 1900, and in 1903 Owens College became the Victoria University of Manchester, though it was often known simply as the University of Manchester, or simpler still 'Owens'. The years between 1890 and 1914 were a key time for the development of the university, which expanded rapidly with new laboratories, and between 1918 and 1939 new arts buildings to the south of Burlington Street were added.

56 The University of Manchester on Oxford Road.

57 The University of Manchester's Sackville Street campus (formerly UMIST).

It was not only through higher education that Manchester displayed intellectual influence. C.P. Scott and the *Manchester Guardian* became highly influential in journalism and the newspaper industry, which continues as the notable London-based *Guardian* newspaper. The *Manchester Guardian* was founded by John Edward Taylor in 1821, and some would argue in response to the demise of the *Manchester Observer*, the rather short-lived radical newspaper that regularly received attention from the authorities, as was outlined in earlier chapters. C.P. Scott began working at the *Manchester Guardian* in 1871, becoming an editor in 1872 and finally taking over as owner by 1905. Scott proved to be highly influential in journalism and took the paper to national and international influence, and it became the most notable provincial newspaper in the country, offering a range of political positions and tackling a range of issues such as Irish Home Rule, opposing British imperialism in South Africa, and women's campaigns for the vote. The paper was seen to be more Liberal in its political leanings and did not shy away from social issues of the time, increasingly reporting on social problems. Scott was regularly seen cycling to and from his home in Fallowfield to central Manchester each day. He retired in 1929, having been editor for fifty-seven years, and three out of his four children went into the family business as managers and editors of the paper. In 1930, he was given the freedom of the city of Manchester, though shortly after, on 1 January 1932, he passed away. The newspaper remained the *Manchester Guardian* until 1959 where it continued as the national *Guardian*.

Working-class Life

Class-based distinctions were ever present during the Edwardian phase and, despite living standards and wages generally rising during this time, life was very much based on working class versus middle class as it was during the nineteenth century. Gender distinctions between men as the breadwinners and women in domestic roles were also still apparent. The male working-class world revolved around work, the pub and drinking at their local, often gambling, and sport, particularly football, which by the Edwardian phase had become a chief Saturday afternoon activity. The pub and drink was a male occupation in every sense, where men networked and where women were actively excluded from certain parts of pubs. Football also excluded women. Often families were pitched into poverty, not necessarily because of lack of earnings, but because of the breadwinner spending the family earnings in pubs, which was a source of conflict in many northern working-class homes. Women's leisure time was spent either in their home or with other women, visiting the cinema which was a newly developing form of leisure, as film as a form of entertainment emerged, and visits to the music hall.[18] Trips to the seaside were also becoming popular, as paid holidays were now a part of working life, and bank holidays enabled the occasional extra day off, facilitated by the Bank Holidays Act of 1871, though it was not until 1938, after a 20-year campaign, that paid holidays were introduced. The railways provided opportunities for the urban population of Manchester to go to such places as the seaside, and resorts such as Blackpool developed, though Southport was more of a middle-class destination. Closer to home, Belle Vue remained a key working-class visitor attraction, as was White City near Old Trafford, which was the original site of the Art Treasures Exhibition in 1857 but by 1907 had become an amusement park, and by the 1920s and 1930s had developed into a motorcycle speedway and greyhound track.[19]

Sport, in particular football, was one of the most popular leisure activities and the city is well known for hosting two of the footballing giants that have a long and fascinating history and tradition. Of course, we are talking about Manchester United and Manchester City! We are all familiar with Manchester United's home of Old Trafford on the edge of Manchester city centre. However, their origins were in Newton Heath and they formed in 1878 as Newton Heath Lancashire and Yorkshire Railway. As the name implies, workers of local industries who were keen on football often formed competitive teams. Often, teams were based at their local pub, which provided a base and basic facilities such as changing rooms. The rash of teams from this era merged eventually to form a football league in 1888. Ironically, the Newton Heath team did not join the league at the start due to concerns about their talent, but they eventually joined the fold in 1892. At the turn of the twentieth century, United faced financial difficulties that almost put them out of business until local brewer, John Davies, came to the rescue. Davies saw a business opportunity and agreed to invest in the club in return for a stake in its operations. This turned it into the successful club that we associate with today. First, the name was changed to Manchester United. Ernest Mangnall was appointed secretary in September 1903 but was also their first manager, and made a number of signings such as goalkeeper Harry Moger and forward Charlie Sagar that led to them performing well in the league, finishing third in the Second Division in both the 1903/04 and 1904/05 seasons. They did even better in the 1905/06 season when they reached the quarter-finals of the FA Cup and finished as runners-up in the Second Division. The signing of Billy Meredith proved to be a particularly wise move and ensured that they won the league title in 1907/08. By this time they were one of the best clubs in the country. The following season they relocated to the Old Trafford ground, which had been purchased by the Manchester Brewery Company and leased back to the club. The outbreak of the First World War led to the suspension of the league until 1919 and by this time Billy Meredith was still at the club, but in the latter stages of his career and making fewer appearances. United finished twelfth in the First Division at the end of this first post-war season and there was a new hero in Joe Spence, the club's most prolific goal scorer of this time. By 1920, Ernest Magnall had moved to Manchester City, taking Meredith with him. United were relegated in their first season without him, winning only eight of their forty-two matches in 1921/22, but a couple of seasons later their fortunes began to improve.[20]

The history of Manchester City football club very much mirrors that of United, beginning around 1880 at St Mark's Church in Gorton. They, like United, took part in local competitions and in 1887 the team became Ardwick AFC and move to a ground on Hyde Road. In 1892, the Second Division of the English Football League was formed and Ardwick AFC was one of its founding members. By 1894, they had become Manchester City Football Club and in 1899 won the league. Further success came in 1904 when they beat Bolton Wanderers in the FA Cup final to become the first Manchester side to win a major event. However, it was not all plain sailing, since in 1906 there were problems with financial irregularities which resulted in the suspension of seventeen players and captain Billy Meredith, who had moved across the city to Manchester United, though Meredith later returned to City. It was a fire at City's Hyde Road ground in the early 1920s that resulted in their move to Maine Road.[21]

Conclusion

Edwardian Manchester was a time of transition, both economically and culturally. The city was faced with a profound need for regeneration as the cotton industry markedly declined and the lead-up to war meant that Manchester was well placed to develop engineering industries, mainly at the rapidly developing Trafford Park area, to foster new skills and employment opportunities as well as being key for the war effort during the First World War. The city centre held a new civic pride, with modern architecture blending in with Victorian opulence. Politically, intellectually and culturally the city was at the heart of campaigns for women's voting rights, academic endeavour and the rise of football as a predominant form of working-class leisure, particularly through its two famous football teams. Unfortunately, war was on the horizon again, and this is the focus of the next part of the story.

Notes

1 Pankhurst, E., *My Own Story* (Hesperus Classics, 2015), ch. 1.

2 Kidd, *Manchester*, p. 182–3.

3 Pankhurst, *My Own Story*.

4 Stevenson, *British Society*, p. 228.

5 Stevenson, *British Society*, p. 27.

6 George, A.D., 'A Note on A V Roe and the Brownsfield Mill, Ancoats, *Manchester Region History Review*, vol. 7. (1993), pp. 93–6.

7 manchesterairport.co.uk

8 Stevenson, *British Society*, p. 51.

9 Stedman, M., *Manchester PALS* (Leo Cooper, 2004).

10 Stedman, *Manchester PALS*, ch. 9.

11 Simon, *A Century*, p. 119.

12 Stevenson, *British Society*, p. 235.

13 Wildman, C., *The Spectacle of Interwar Manchester and Liverpool: urban fantasies, consumer cultures and gendered Identities* (PhD thesis, University of Manchester, 2007), p. 32.

14 Stevenson, *British Society*, p. 222.

15 Wildman, *The Spectacle*, p. 37.

16 Stevenson, *British Society*, p. 227.

17 Simon, *A Century*, pp. 280–1.

18 Davies, A., Fielding, S., *Workers' Worlds: cultures and communities in Manchester & Salford, 1880 – 1939* (Manchester University Press, 1992).

19 Jennison, G., Zoological Gardens, Belle Vue, Manchester (1929).

20 Taken from manutd.com

21 Taken from mancity.com

nine

LOWRY'S MANCHESTER

I saw the industrial scene and I was affected by it. I tried to paint it all the time.
I tried to paint the industrial scene as best I could. It wasn't easy.

L.S. Lowry (1930s)

Introduction

L.S. Lowry captured life in post-war Manchester and neighbouring Salford like no other. His portrayal of industrial scenes, street life and working-class trips to work, football and other aspects of everyday existence have become an iconic record of Mancunian working-class life. But what was life like in Lowry's Manchester? This chapter looks at Manchester from the onset of war in 1939, when conflict again came to the city – and this time quite literally, as parts of central Manchester were destroyed in air raids – through the post-war period of reconstruction to the economic hardship of the 1970s. Before and during the war, it was a time of rationing and often poverty, and out of post-war reconstruction emerged a city that was struggling in the wake of unemployment as many manufacturing industries continued to decline. However, by the end of the 1970s Manchester started to gain confidence in itself once more. Higher education became one of its key strengths, following on from the development of the University of Manchester, and continuing with the development of technical colleges that ultimately became institutions of higher education in their own right. The birth of the NHS took place in one of Manchester's local hospitals; and there was shopping like never before, with the construction of the Arndale Centre and its famous yellow-tiled exterior. This period was a tough one, but one which laid the foundations for future prosperity.

Lowry and Wartime Manchester

L.S. Lowry had a routine day job but he broke out of the mould to follow his creative instincts, to leave us with a fascinating visual record of how Manchester and its people emerged out of post-war austerity to a modern and cosmopolitan city. Born in Stretford in 1887, Lowry's work from the 1920s epitomised the city and region, and works such as *Coming from the Mill* in 1930 and *Going to the Match* of 1953 portrayed how people lived and worked, and many of our northern ancestors totally relate to the often dreariness of ordinary life he captured in his paintings. Lowry was initially raised in the middle-class Manchester suburb of Longsight, but at some point moved to Victoria Park near Rusholme. The family must have fallen on hard times, as they eventually relocated to Pendlebury. He had a tough upbringing, his mother not bonding with him, and even having trouble looking at him at times, because not only did she want a girl, but she found her son very clumsy and hard to relate to. His father was also lacking in the emotion required as a parent. Lowry went to the Manchester School of Art where he studied under the guidance of French painter Pierre Adolphe Valette, who also painted evocative Manchester scenes. Lowry spent over forty years collecting rents for the Pall Mall property company, and his day job largely concealed the talent that was to emerge. When the family moved to Pendlebury, Lowry enrolled at Salford School of Art, now the Peel Building at the University of Salford, and it was the area around Pendlebury that came to dominate much of his artistic work and here he drew some iconic images of the Salford landscape overlooking Peel Park. His style of painting became famous as 'matchstick men', which is shown in Figure 58, his work *Going to Work*, which he produced in 1943.[1] This painting is one example of several he created that very much captures how Manchester came to be perceived, with many working-class people undertaking the daily grind at their local office or factory. Skies were often grey, reflecting Manchester's association with rain. During the war Lowry became a volunteer fire officer and also was appointed as an official war artist in 1943. He died in 1976, aged 88, in Glossop, Derbyshire, and his legacy is secured at the Lowry Gallery in Salford Quays, which displays many of his works.

58 L.S. Lowry, *Going to Work*, 1943. (Copyright the Imperial War Museum)

We have already seen how the Manchester Pals went to the front line in France to fight in the First World War. The Second World War was different in the sense that war came to the city, despite much of the fighting taking place on the European mainland. It has been shown that Heaton Park was an important place for the training of the Manchester Pals regiments and in the Second World War it also had an important role in training the RAF. Why was Manchester bombed, when it was far away from the main fighting arena on mainland Europe? Clearly, the Nazis found it of industrial and strategic importance as a centre for engineering and production. In particular, Trafford Park had become a key manufacturing base not just for the region but the country, particularly with respect to the war effort, and the German intention was to disable Britain's key places that provided infrastructure to the war effort. Air raids began to severely affect the region from June 1940 and the first bombs hit the city in the August and continued through the rest of that year. On 22 and 23 December, for two nights, in what is commonly referred to as the Christmas Blitz, the Royal Exchange in St Ann's Square was struck, and the Free Trade Hall, Cross Street Chapel, Albert Square and Portland Street were all devastated. Manchester Cathedral was also badly affected, and in fact was the second most damaged cathedral in England after Coventry. Even half of Piccadilly was destroyed. Deansgate and Oxford Road were cut off by debris and unexploded bombs, and key utilities such as water supplies and electricity were badly affected. On this occasion, an estimated 680 died and 2,000 were injured, with a further 6,000 finding themselves homeless. Around 72,000 children and 23,000 adults were forced to evacuate the city.[2] In total, the Manchester Blitz affected around 30,000 homes in the region. There were other smaller air raids as well, and one of the worst of these was in June 1941. Figure 59 shows the damage inflicted near the Royal Exchange, where the tower can be seen in the background. Despite the devastation, the town hall, Central Library and the Midland Hotel escaped damage, and there is an ongoing story that Hitler purposefully omitted the Midland Hotel from the raids, with some historians suggesting that there is evidence that it was not on their lists of targets simply because Hitler wanted the Midland Hotel as Nazi headquarters in post-war Britain, should they have won the war.[3]

The Manchester Blitz caused much damage to the basic infrastructure of the city, with many warehouses destroyed and transport connections badly affected, with two of the main train stations and local bus stations damaged. The last large-scale air raid took place in August 1942.

59   Bomb damage in central Manchester, 1940. (Copyright Imperial War Museum)

Engineering skills at Avro were vital to the war effort, just as they had been during the First World War, and the RAF were especially keen on the company's Manchester bomber, Lancaster and Lincoln aeroplanes. By this time, Avro had a number of sites around the Manchester area that built these vital wartime aircraft, including Chadderton, near Oldham, and Woodford, near Stockport. Trafford Park was vital for the country's industrial war effort, where, for example, Metropolitan Vickers electrical engineering was located, where they produced equipment such as generators and turbines. It was one of the largest and most important engineering companies of its time and was a world leader in its field. Unfortunately this made Trafford Park an attractive target to the Germans and was struck in bombing raids during December 1940 and again in 1941 when Manchester United's ground at Old Trafford was also devastated, as the main stand and some back offices were destroyed. The football league had already been suspended but until their ground was fully operational again they played home games at Maine Road, home to their local rivals Manchester City.

Post-War Manchester – Reconstruction and Decline

The last chapter showed how, during the Edwardian era, there were plans to remove the old slums and build better housing that incorporated more open spaces in the city. Even during the Second World War these plans remained in place despite the devastation to the city centre. In 1945, a plan was published by city surveyor, Roland Nicholas, which provided the basis for discussion on what form the future of the city's planning and architecture should take. It was evident in this report that the preservation of Manchester's architectural heritage was not top of the list of priorities, since the Manchester Corporation clearly wanted to remove references to its Victorian past, largely because of its association with poverty, poor housing and ill health. Additionally, there was also little recognition of the finer buildings the Victorians had built, and even more alarmingly recent evidence had been uncovered that indicates there were discussions about the potential demolition of Manchester Town Hall.[4] However, Nicholas's plans were somewhat ambitious and the cost prevented much of it being implemented. Despite post-war economic uncertainty, many of the city's finer buildings that had been destroyed in the Blitz were reconstructed. The Free Trade Hall was little more than a shell but it was rebuilt behind the remaining façade and sympathetically restored, and reopened as a concert hall in 1951. The Royal Exchange was repaired and opened again in 1953, though the new Exchange was a scaled-down version of its predecessor, in line with the cotton industry's decline, and closed as a trading exchange in 1968. Cross Street Chapel was rebuilt and opened again by 1959.

After the Second World War, the cotton industry was little more than a minor issue in industrial terms. If the First World War marked the initial nail, the Second World War was certainly the final nail in the industry's coffin. This was particularly bad news for Manchester which, coming out of wartime destruction and facing the economic realities of reconstruction, now lacked the economic base that had made the city famous, with little to replace it in the short term. Central government were ploughing most of their post-war finances in the southern part of the country and Manchester was not alone in this situation, in which the former industrial bases of northern cities had been hard hit and were now counting the cost of the war, with central-government resources being ploughed into London and the south-east. However, despite this rather gloomy economic picture, nearby Trafford Park continued to provide employment opportunities in sectors such as engineering that had been so vital during the war effort. By the late 1960s, around 50,000 people were employed on the site, but even these impressive figures disguised fluctuations in the post-war economic climate, and employment opportunities fluctuated with it. The role of Trafford Park in manufacturing and engineering had peaked in 1945 following the wartime effort, when around 75,000 people were employed by the end of the war. However, companies started to leave Trafford Park for newer premises elsewhere. By the end of the 1960s, employment had fallen to around 50,000 and continued to decline over the course of the 1970s. During the post-war period, Avro maintained production of reconnaissance aircraft as global politics remained volatile and a nuclear cold war threat loomed. By the 1960s, the Avro name disappeared as the company became part of Hawker Siddeley Aviation Limited. However, there was nostalgia attached to the Avro name and many did not want to it see disappearing into eternity, and it did indeed return when, by the 1990s, the company became British Aerospace, and one of their jets was named the A.V. Roe RJ.[5]

Between the 1960s and 1980s, Manchester was showing signs of severe economic depression. Many local mills, that had become huge white elephants once the cotton industry had disappeared, were being converted to other such uses as engineering plants and new mail order companies, which saw a

60   The Co-operative Insurance Building – the CIS as it is commonly known.

new usage for these large Victorian monoliths, which Nicholas's urban redevelopment plans could not afford to remove. Here, companies such as the engineering firm Ferranti began developing old mills, with four of their plants sited in former cotton mills. Trade via the Manchester Ship Canal had peaked, in terms of the volume of goods being carried, in the late 1950s, but the city was still one of the UK largest ports. However, it began to lose momentum as container ships became larger, and which the canal could not support, and by 1982 it closed as a port. Heavier industries never recovered their pre-wartime position and during the 1970s and 1980s Manchester lost tens of thousands of jobs, mainly in the manufacturing sector. In 1966, Central Station was closed in consequence of the Beeching plan of the 1960s that destroyed a great deal of the railway system, and in 1975 Liverpool Road goods depot was also shut. Despite this, some businesses were doing well, and this was reflected in new buildings, the most notable of which was the Co-operative Insurance Building on Miller Street, which was completed in 1962 by Sir John Burnet and at the time was the tallest office block in Europe, and designed to make a statement about the success of the Co-operative Group.[6]

Post-War Innovation

However, despite the economic uncertainties there were other aspects of Manchester's economy and technological developments that were moving rapidly, and this is seen in the expansion of higher education that began to produce a number of innovations that would have global impact. First, the former College of Technology became the University of Manchester Institute of Science and Technology (UMIST) in the mid-1960s, though despite its name it was largely independent of the University of Manchester until their merger in 2004. John Dalton College of Technology opened in 1964, and the Domestic and Trades College, also known as Hollings College opened in 1960. We have already seen how the University of Manchester had become one of the most well-established institutions of its kind in the country. By the post-war period it could boast of a number of great and Nobel Prize-winning academics. After 1945, the science, engineering and medical departments were relocated to the east of Oxford Road. The John Rylands Library on Deansgate, which had started out as one of the world's finest charity libraries, joined the university in 1972. Additionally, another of the region's great cultural centres, the Whitworth

61 The Whitworth Art Gallery.

Art Gallery, joined the university in 1958.[7] The Whitworth was founded in 1889 to commemorate Sir Joseph Whitworth, a notable Manchester engineer, whose legacy funded many of Manchester's educational investments around the beginning of the twentieth century.

The university became noted for attracting some of the brightest academics of their generation. For example, the historian A.J.P. Taylor lectured at the university between 1930 and 1938. Taylor, a sometimes controversial academic, published widely on nineteenth-century European diplomatic history, and later became a television personality. One of the most intellectually acclaimed academics was Ernest Rutherford, who was Professor of Physics at the university from 1907. Originally from New Zealand, Rutherford was born in 1871. His academic life took him initially to Cambridge and then subsequently he became Chair of Physics at McGill University in Montreal. He returned to England in 1907 to take up the Manchester post of Langworthy Professor of Physics. Another important academic was Max Newman, a mathematician who is noted for his Second World War code-breaking abilities and who had invented the Colossus computer. He was appointed Chair of Mathematics at the University of Manchester in 1945, and by 1946 he was securing funds to create a computing machine laboratory, which was funded by the Royal Society. Shortly afterwards, Frederic Williams and Tom Kilburn joined the department and the research that this team produced has had a profound effect on computing as a discipline. Freddie Williams first obtained his degree in engineering at the University of Manchester and later gained a doctorate at Oxford, and after this he returned to Manchester to take up a lecturing position. He was soon working alongside mathematician Tom Kilburn. Alan Turing, who many regard as the father of modern computing, and was the mathematical genius credited with breaking the Nazi enigma codes and shortening the war, joined the university's mathematics department in 1948 until 1951. The technology that had been developed in the Second World War had a major impact on how technology would work in society in the future and Max Newman and Alan Turing's work was especially influential. In 1948, Manchester gave birth to 'Baby', the development of the first computer, which marked the start of an information technology revolution. The Manchester Small-Scale Experimental Machine, which was nicknamed Baby, was the first example in the world where a programme was stored in a computer memory rather than on paper or other mechanism, and heralded the arrival of modern computing that has continued to evolve and that we so heavily rely on today. The collaboration between Freddie Williams, Tom Kilburn and the team was instrumental in making this happen.

62 Replica of *Baby* at the Museum of Science and Industry. (Courtesy of Alamy)

63 Statue of Alan Turing in Sackville Park.

Some years later, Kilburn developed the first computer department in the country at the university, where in October 1964 the newly created Department of Computing began the first ever degree course in computer science, when twenty-eight students gained places. The department established a long and fruitful relationship with the engineering company Ferranti, and the first commercial computer was sold by them in 1951. Turing worked on the Mark 1 computer, the next stage of computing, that was a higher-specification version of Baby and was in use by 1949. A statue of Alan Turing can be found in Sackville Park, close to the university's Sackville Street campus, and a working replica of Baby can be seen in Manchester's Museum of Science and Industry.

Since the 1950s, the construction of the Lovell telescope at Jodrell Bank in the Cheshire countryside has done much to further astronomy. Bernard Lovell arrived at the University's physics department in 1945 to study cosmic rays, and his attempts at developing a telescope on Oxford Road were hindered by background noise and interference, so he set about finding a quieter place that was sufficiently remote that the telescope's performance would not be affected. When construction was complete in 1957, the telescope was the largest steerable dish radio telescope in the world, and it is still the third largest. Lovell's work on telescopes, and the profile of Jodrell Bank as an astronomy facility, remains world renown.[8]

Moving away from higher education to government policy, the Labour Party was elected in 1945 on a manifesto to rebuild the much damaged home front after the wartime devastation. Part of their policy was to implement health care for all and was based on recommendations from the 1942 Beveridge Report. This report was the catalyst that led to the formation of the new National Health Service (NHS) which was effectively born in Manchester. On 5 July 1948, Bevan officially launched the NHS at the Park Hospital in Manchester, which was the first to be opened as part of the NHS. In 1988, Park Hospital was renamed Trafford General to mark the 40th anniversary of the start of the NHS and its role in the history of the service. Manchester hospitals have also been at the forefront of cancer treatment, notably via the world famous Christie Hospital. Its origins can be found at the end of the nineteenth century when Sir Joseph Whitworth bequeathed money for good causes. One of these was to Richard Christie, who established the hospital. The Christie became part of the NHS at the start in 1948 and has become a world leader in cancer care. The Manchester Royal Infirmary (MRI) and nearby Manchester Eye Hospital are also two leaders in their field and have strong roots in the city. MRI began

64 The Lovell Telescope at Jodrell Bank.

as a small hospital in Withy Grove in 1752, established by Charles White and Joseph Bancroft. It soon outgrew the site and through Oswald Mosely, who donated land in Piccadilly, a new hospital was built which opened in 1755. It was in 1908 that the MRI moved to its present location on Oxford Road with the site being chosen because of its proximity to the university's medical school. It also became part of the NHS in 1948. The Manchester Eye Hospital has a similar history in that interest and innovation in the nineteenth century led to the desire to open a facility dedicated to diseases of the eyes, and in 1814 James Wilson started the process of creating a centre on King Street. It subsequently moved to Faulkner Street in 1827 and Princess Street in 1874. The first eye surgeon was appointed in 1883, and a year later it relocated to its present site on Oxford Road.

Cultural Identity

Manchester was shaping a twentieth-century cultural identity, both in terms of highbrow pursuits but also through its largely working-class sporting endeavours. Music in particular has played a prominent part of Manchester's cultural heritage. For example, the Royal Northern College of Music is one of the leading institutions of its kind, and its roots can be traced back into the late nineteenth century with the creation of the Royal Manchester College of Music. It was the initial idea of Charles Hallé, who had developed the Hallé Orchestra and entertained the concept of a music college. After some fundraising, the music college opened in 1893 with Hallé as the principal, and Queen Victoria conferring royal status. In 1920, a northern school of music was established and for a time both music schools were separate and coexisted, and it was not until 1955 that both college principals met to discuss the idea of a merger, though it was not until 1967 that plans were put in place to achieve this, and in 1972 the Royal Northern College of Music began, moving to its current site on Oxford Road in 1973.[9]

Sir Charles Hallé and his Hallé Orchestra performed for the first time in 1857 as part of the Art Treasures Exhibition. Hallé himself was a regular conductor and pianist until his death in 1895, but his passing was not the end of the orchestra, as his legacy continued through some close friends. Until the outbreak of the Second World War, the home of the Hallé was the Free Trade Hall, but the wartime bombing which devastated the hall meant that the orchestra moved to a variety of locations. By 1951, the Free Trade Hall had been reopened and the Hallé moved back there until 1996 when it relocated to a new home at the Bridgewater Hall. One of the orchestra's most influential conductors was Sir John Barbirolli, who began work with the orchestra in 1943 and stayed for some twenty-seven years. Barbirolli was born in London to Italian and French parents who were also both fine musicians. He entered the London Trinity College of Music at just 10 years old. After joining the army in the First World War, his post-war career began in earnest in conducting orchestras and playing in the London Symphony Orchestra as well as others. He served as conductor of the Scottish Orchestra in Glasgow and the New York Philharmonic. He arrived in Manchester in 1943, in the middle of the Second World War and effectively recreated the Hallé from scratch. He had problems keeping an orchestra

65 Statue of John Barbirolli outside the Bridgewater Hall.

of any quality together during the war but his persistence kept the orchestra going even during this difficult time. He took the Hallé Orchestra from strength to strength, putting on local concerts and touring throughout the UK and overseas. His tenure came to an end in 1970 with his death, but his legacy remains.[10]

'I Was There!'

At the other end of the musical spectrum was popular music and a youth culture that had a marked effect on the city. In fact, one of the most notable punk concerts of its generation was performed by the Sex Pistols in June 1976. It took place at the Lesser Free Trade Hall, a smaller room within the Free Trade Hall, and has been labelled one of the most important concerts of all time by many, and in fact by far more than the forty who were actually supposed to be there, claiming 'I was there'. Those who were definitely at the concert included Mark E. Smith, who later developed the careers of The Fall, Morrissey and Tony Wilson of Factory Records fame. The Pistols held a follow-up concert six weeks later and here future Simply Red singer Mick Hucknall, whose early work was very much influenced by punk, 'was there'. It was a catalyst for laying the foundations of the music scene that was to come in the 1990s and 2000s. Whatever London could produce, Manchester could do it much better! Despite the Pistols concerts being small events, costing a mere 50 pence to attend, they have been acclaimed as being as culturally significant as Woodstock and Live Aid. Here it was not about numbers, but musical influences that helped to shape the music scene for a generation, including the Buzzcocks, the Happy Mondays and Oasis.[11]

However, things were not going too well for another of Manchester's forms of leisure as Belle Vue became a casualty of decline and financial problems. It has already been shown how the amusement park and zoo was such a feature of nineteenth century and Edwardian working-class leisure. Despite its financial ups and downs over the decades, it managed to survive, but this time the end was real, and in 1988 the site finally closed its doors. During the 1950s and 1960s, Belle Vue had something of a renaissance but by the end of the 1960s things started to deteriorate as competing leisure pursuits led to a massive reduction in visitor numbers. Sir Leslie Joseph and Charles Forte purchased the park in 1956, though by 1963 Forte owned it outright. In 1958, the park was devastated by fire that narrowly missed the zoo. It recovered from this but by the 1970s things started to go awry and the site was making huge losses.

Despite initially only parts of the park closing in a bid to turn it around, and only opening at weekends, the end was inevitable and the park closed. Maud the Tigon, one of the famous inhabitants of Belle Vue and which died in 1949, has been preserved and is one of the exhibits at Manchester Museum.

Another aspect of Manchester's cultural identity is the longest-running television soap opera *Coronation Street*, and the fictional working-class community of Weatherfield has adorned our screens since December 1960. The programme was the brainchild of Granada TV scriptwriter Tony Warren. Starting out as a pilot with a handful of episodes, it soon gained popular appeal, with its depictions of northern working-class life centred around the Rovers Return public house, the local corner shop, a factory and inhabitants in houses that are synonymous with Manchester's working class. It has entertained millions, and its strong characters such as Ena Sharples, Ken Barlow (portrayed by William Roache, the longest-running character in the show) and his wife Deirdre, Rita and Mavis in the corner shop, and Bett Lynch, the busty blonde barmaid at the Rovers Return are just a handful of the characters who have made the show what it is. Its success has been attributed to a mix of ordinary working-class lives combined with a wit and humour in its varied storylines that are not afraid to confront controversial societal issues. *Coronation Street* has always been at home in Granada TV studios, which was built in 1956 on Quay Street, marking the start of a post-war medium that was to become a feature of most people's homes. ITV moved in 2013 to MediaCity at Salford Quays and here the set of *Coronation Street* relocated.

Post-war football saw the rise of Manchester's two teams to even greater success. Reconstruction at Manchester United not only led to a rebuilt ground but a new manager in the form of Matt Busby, who proved to be one of the most notable figures in MUFC's history. He commenced in 1945 and in unprecedented fashion continued until the 1970s. His team became affectionately known as the Busby Babes, a young, highly talented and very successful team. Busby came from Scotland, but had played at Manchester City and was part of their 1934 FA Cup winning side. He had also played at Liverpool, but his interests lay in joining Manchester United and working with Walter Crickmer, the former manager and club secretary when Busby joined the club. They were both instrumental in developing a team from their junior players and within two years they had won their first competition for over forty years when in 1948 they secured the FA cup against Blackpool. The Busby Babes went on to win a number of cup and league titles. However, their success was brutally

66 Manchester United Football Club at Old Trafford. (Courtesy of Alamy)

cut short when, on 6 February 1958, returning from a European cup tie, their plane crashed on the runway at Munich Airport. Seven players – Geoff Bent, Roger Byrne, Eddie Colman, Mark Jones, David Pegg, Tommy Taylor and Billy Whelan – and three club officials were initially killed alongside fourteen others. Duncan Edwards died from his injuries two weeks later. Two further players were never able to play football again. Busby was badly injured and was lucky to survive. During the 1960s, Busby, after recovering from very severe injuries in the air disaster, was faced with the task of building a young and vibrant team once more. Dennis Viollet, Bill Foulkes and Bobby Charlton all survived the crash and were joined by a set of new signings. The club's results were some-what erratic to begin with, but in 1962 the signing of George Best marked the start of a new era of footballers as stars in their own right attracting non-footballing media attention. In the 1964/65 and 1966/67 seasons they won the league title. In 1968, the team won the European Cup and Matt Busby was knighted.[12]

Over at Maine Road, Manchester City former captain Sam Cowan became their manager in 1946, and like Busby was part of a new generation of keen and motivated managers. During his early days MCFC won nineteen matches on the run without defeat. However, Cowan decided to relinquish his role in 1947. MCFC made a controversial decision in 1949 with the signing of Bert

Trautmann, the German goalkeeper who had not returned to his native country after the war. Any prejudice against him was soon lost and he became a key player and a firm favourite, and by the end of his career he was praised as being one the greatest ever goalkeepers. In 1956, they won the FA Cup final, and this game is also remembered for Trautmann continuing to play despite having broken his neck during the game. City were unfortunately relegated in 1963, but returned to the First Division once more in 1966, where they continued with some good form that led them to the league title in 1968, and FA Cup glory in the 1969 season, beating Leicester City. In 1970, they were at the top of their form, winning both the European Cup Winners Cup and the League Cup.[13]

Conclusion

The time from the start of the Second World War to the 1970s was one of ups and downs in the fortunes of Manchester's economy and its development. The Blitz did much damage to city centre, and post-war regeneration was difficult. Aspiration and plans did not match the budgets that were available to northern cities for urban redevelopment. From the initial post-war period until the 1970s, Manchester faced a range of problems in reconstructing its economy and industrial base, and suffered economic depression and fluctuating employment levels in the wake of traditional industries dying and trying to forge a new economic focus. Central Manchester and nearby Trafford Park took the full force of German bombing, but in the post-war era many of its historic buildings were restored to their former glory. The post-1945 grand plans for the city centre thankfully never came off, since had they been achieved much of the city's Victorian heritage would have been destroyed. However, culturally and scientifically, Manchester forged ahead. In the fields of science and innovation, Manchester University was at the forefront of development that would have a profound effect not only on the disciplines of computer science and physics but on how society has changed in consequence of living with such technologies. Culturally, the region enjoyed an eclectic mix of music. Thus, the era was a mixture of great problems but also great achievements. The story now moves on to look at the 1980s to the 2000 where Manchester's cosmopolitan culture really begins to have a global impact, and brings Manchester's history to the present day.

Notes

1 Leber, M., 'The Remarkable Legacy of L S Lowry', *Manchester Region History Review*, vol. 1(2) (1987), pp. 13–22.

2 http://www.manchestereveningnews.co.uk/news/greater-manchester-news/manchester-blitz-bomb-sites-map-10465447 [accesses 28 December 2016]; http://www.iwm.org.uk/history/the-manchester-blit

3 http://www.manchestereveningnews.co.uk/news/greater-manchester-news/manchester-christmas-blitz-hitler-boms-10622931 [accessed 28 December 2016].

4 Bamford, P., *Manchester: 50 years of change* (HMSO, 1995).

5 See www.baesystems.com/en/heritage/av-roe---company

6 Coop.co.uk

7 See www.manchester.ac.uk

8 http://www.jb.man.ac.uk/history/early.html

9 rncm.ac.uk

10 barbirollisociety.co.uk

11 Haslam, D., *Manchester: the story of the pop cult city* (Fourth Estate, 1999).

12 See www.manutd.com/en/History.aspx

13 See www.mancity.com/en/fans-and-community/club/club-history

ten

THE MADCHESTER YEARS

First famed and feared a hundred and fifty years ago, as it became the first industrial city in the world,
Manchester has been reinventing itself for a new century, on an experimental journey from despair to where.

Dave Haslem (1999)

Introduction

Post-war Manchester suffered the effects of economic decline that were preva-lent in the country as a whole. The 1980s, however, marked a turning point in regeneration that has continued. This chapter looks at the phase from the 1980s to the present day, since it is during this period that Manchester has become the vibrant city that it deserves to be. It is a place of modernity and cosmo-politan style and an exciting centre of culture, industry and commerce. The city has faced some major challenges during these latter decades, and none more significant than the effects of the 1996 IRA bombing that physically ripped at the heart of the city, but on a human level created a pulling together of people and businesses. The regeneration that followed created a desire to transform the city centre on an unprecedented scale, which reflected both Manchester's heritage and its desire for modernity, when old buildings and new were repaired and reconstructed with equal care. The youth culture in the city during the 1980s and 1990s has often been referred to as the 'Madchester years', follow-ing on from the 1970s Sex Pistols concerts, where a new nightclub in the form of the Hacienda made a distinct popular cultural impact. Manchester has also been regenerated through its achievements in sporting events and has some of the best facilities, and athletes, in the country. Here, Manchester's story is brought to the present.

The Greater Manchester County

Today, Manchester is more often seen as 'Greater Manchester', not just a city but a county that not only includes the city of Manchester but also incorporates a number of towns that surround it. Here, the nine metropolitan boroughs of Bolton, Bury, Oldham, Rochdale, Salford, Stockport, Tameside, Trafford and Wigan join the City of Manchester as one large urban conurbation. However, this was not always the case, and up to the 1970s Manchester was still a part of Lancashire. In 1972, the Local Government Act was passed and in 1974 two new metropolitan counties were formed, those of Merseyside and Greater Manchester. This new county was run by the Greater Manchester County Council from 1974 and had responsibilities for services such as transport, planning, refuse and so on and was located in a county hall on Portland Street. It was, however, rather short lived since, under the Conservative Government of 1983, their election manifesto was clear in its determination to eradicate many of these metropolitan councils, mainly because they were seen as too costly and so were subsequently disbanded. The Greater Manchester County Council was abolished in 1986 and each metropolitan borough within the county effectively became a unitary authority.[1] However, 'Greater Manchester' is still a recognised geographic area and the term could be used more as a generic form to describe the area than having the formal role that it once had.

Regeneration

Manchester has enjoyed a sustained period of regeneration since the 1980s and some of this was symptomatic of an empty place in the economy where Manchester's natural industrial base had declined rapidly with little to replace it. It was also a consequence of the economic depression that many of Britain's cities suffered in the 1970s, in particular, inner-city areas where poorly built high-rise housing estates, combined with unemployment, created a range of social problems. However, the government introduced measures to end this downward spiral, and one of their policies was the creation of urban corporations. In the 1980s, Manchester Council created the Castlefield Conservation Area to redevelop the historic site which had fallen into obscurity. Here, plans were put in place to develop the former fort into a Roman garden which included reconstruction of the North Gate that was described in Chapter One. By 1982, Castlefield had become the country's first urban heritage park. Just across the road from Castlefield's Roman site is the former Liverpool Road Station and in 1983 the first stages of the newly created Museum of Science and Industry were completed, utilising the former goods depot, and again resurrecting the area's heritage in recognising the world's first passenger railway station, which had seen the first train run to Liverpool in 1830. In addition to these, in 1986, the old central railway station was converted into the GMEX, becoming England's largest single exhibition hall, and over recent years has hosted a number of political party conferences and trade and cultural exhibitions as well as the odd pop concert. The political party conferences that had always been traditionally held in seaside resorts turned their attention to major cities of the UK to host their events, alternating each year between Labour and the Conservatives, taking place in the city at the expense of resorts such as Blackpool and Brighton. The GMEX is an innovative and creative use of a redundant building, and even the car park is a historic reminder of the building's former past as the cobbles and rail tracks still sit below the low arches that form the car parking spaces.[2]

The Central Manchester Development Corporation (CMDC) was established in 1988 to secure investment for the city. One of the projects that the CMDC part funded, alongside Manchester Council and the European Regional Development Fund, was the Bridgewater Hall, which was complete in 1996. This new concert venue hosted its first event in September of that year and was officially opened by the Queen in December 1996, and became the home of the Hallé Orchestra (moving from their former base at the Free Trade Hall), the BBC Philarmonic and the Camerata. It is very much associated with classical musical events and is specially designed to provide the best acoustic experience. For some time, it has also been the venue for graduation ceremonies of the Manchester Metropolitan University.

There has been an expansion in higher education in the region that has made it one of the largest concentrations of students outside London. The Greater Manchester region has three universities: the historic University of Manchester, Manchester Metropolitan University and the University of

67 The Bridgewater Hall.

Salford. Teacher training has been a prominent part of education provision in Manchester and at one time there were four colleges in the city offering courses in teacher education. One of these, located in Didsbury, became part of Manchester Polytechnic, which was formed in 1970 following an amalgamation of a number of different institutions, and by the 1980s had become one of the biggest higher education institutions of its kind. In 1992, it achieved university status as the Manchester Metropolitan University. In 2004, both the University of Manchester and UMIST merged to become one of the largest universities in the country and is now amongst the elite 'Russell Group' universities. Along with the University of Salford, the Manchester region has one of the largest and most vibrant learning centres and student population in the country.

Manchester is a consumer delight, and hosts a great many high street and designer names, and much of this is channelled through the Arndale Centre, which is one of the largest shopping centres in Europe. It was designed to be the largest under-cover shopping centre in Europe when construction began in 1972 and designed to house the major retailers of the high street. It cost in the region of £100 million and located on a large 15-acre site which housed a bus station on Cannon Street, parking, offices, and even some flats. It began as a great move for the city's redevelopment and modernisation, but it did have its down side in that many old streets and buildings were demolished, and the resulting centre was certainly no architectural marvel. Some described it as a giant box full of shops and the yellow-tiled exterior made it the butt of jokes. 'The largest public lavatory in the world' was one favourite. Even today there are glimpses of the yellow tiles on the Arndale Tower, which smacks of its 1970s architectural origins, for which many old buildings suffered demolition. It also marked the decay of Oldham Street, which up until the Arndale Centre was built was the key shopping street for high street retailers, and has never fully recovered its former glory days. Even worse was the fire that struck Woolworth's department store at the corner of Oldham Street and Piccadilly on 8 May 1979 in which ten people tragically lost their lives and many more needed hospital treatment. An electrical problem led to some furniture catching fire in a building that had no sprinkler system.

Further afield, Trafford Park was also in need of regeneration as many of the heavier industries had left and the Ship Canal was not required to distribute goods as it had in the past. Whilst the Trafford Centre shopping and

68 Arial view of the Trafford Centre. (Courtesy of Alamy)

leisure complex is some 5 miles outside the city centre, it has transformed shopping for many. It opened in 1998 and is one of the largest shopping complexes in the country. Located at Dumplington, and close to the Trafford Park industrial site and the M60 orbital motorway, it regenerated an area that had fallen into decay. There were concerns over its effects on retailing in both central Manchester and other local towns, but after deliberations and consultations, the House of Lords gave the go-ahead to this initiative. Its success lies in the vast population that live within a reasonable distance of it, and it offers, over and above shopping, opulent architecture and eating experiences from around the Orient, and one of the UK's busiest cinemas, and new additions of Barton Square, a Sea Life Centre and exhibition facilities at Event City. Close by is the skiing experience of the Chill Factore. A visitor who has some understanding of Manchester's historic past cannot fail to notice the marked transition between old and new, from industry to lavish consumerism and impressive architecture.

The CMDC ceased in 1996, but this did not prevent investment rolling into the city. Old warehouses and buildings were restored for a new usage, canals were cleaned up and a new café culture was born, with apartments that reflected a new cosmopolitan era. However, within weeks of the end of the CMDC, the centre of Manchester was devastated by an IRA bomb. At 11.20 a.m. on 15 June 1996, an explosive device went off outside Marks and Spencer on Cross Street. Over 200 were injured but amazingly there were no fatalities. At 9.40 a.m. a warning had been phoned through to Granada TV that led to the area being cleared. Marks and Spencer's store took the full force of the blast but even further away glass windows were shattered in the Royal Exchange, Corn Exchange, cathedral, St Ann's Church, the Chetham's complex and other local buildings. However, some things did survive, and despite the bomb exploding at its side, the post box in Figure 69 is a testament to the survival and regeneration of Manchester. A Lord Mayor's emergency appeal was created and it was amazing how the city responded. Some traders were back in action within a month and Lewis's department store made space for Marks and Spencer until their new store was complete. Competition became cooperation. The bombing kickstarted a city centre master plan like no other, with a competition to generate new ideas for the architecture and layout of the damaged centre. Cannon Street disappeared altogether, along with its bus station and many of the hated yellow tiles, in a redevelopment of the Arndale Centre, creating a fantastic modern shopping space.

69 The postbox on Cross Street that survived the 1996 bombing – a symbol of Manchester's resilience.

70 The redeveloped Arndale Centre.

71 The Old Wellington Inn and Sinclair's Oyster Bar, part of the post-bombing Exchange Square redevelopment.

Marks and Spencer came back bigger than ever, opening in 1999. The walkway that once linked the Arndale Centre to the Marks and Spencer store was restored, and Exchange Square was created. The Old Wellington Inn, the one building that has seen the story of Manchester unfold from its medieval origins, and by this time had survive two bombings (since it also narrowly missed being devastated in the Second World War) was literally moved 400 yards from its former location in the Shambles to just behind the Cathedral. Unfortunately, there is little to remind us of the Shambles itself, which was a victim of the redevelopments. Currently, Marks and Spencer shares its space with Selfridges department store as part of an area that contains some of the finest designer shops along the newly created New Cathedral Street.

'Madchester'

The post-1996 reconstruction of the city centre not only replaced and restored damaged buildings but it also reinforced Manchester's cultural identity as a place for the arts, entertainment and heritage. Manchester as a place for music and youth culture continued throughout the 1980s and 1990s, and the city was coined 'Madchester' as the Hacienda, during its day probably the most famous nightclub in the world, opened in May 1982 in a run-down part of Whitworth Street. The Hacienda arrived at the end of the 1970s punk era and in some respects had an identity crisis since it did not suit the disco scene that was also popular in clubs at this time. However, it was in pole position as the band New Order began to succeed and a new rave culture swept the country. Factory Records owner Tony Wilson, along with New Order and others, came up with the idea of opening a club that represented a new taste in music and clubbing. Its architecture was grittier than previous nightclubs, with an almost industrial feel of wide open space, black and yellow stripes and iron girders. The club struggled for a while, partly because the team managing it had lots of enthusiasm and fascination for new forms of music but had little business acumen. During its life it was the home of acid house music and hosted a number of artists, some of them early in their careers and relatively unknown at the time but who became global successes such as Madonna, the Stone Roses and the Happy Mondays. DJs included Dave Haslem, Mike Pickering and Graeme Park. However, during the 1990s the club was beset with issues of drugs and gang violence and it was after a drugs-related death and shootings that the Hacienda closed in June 1997. FAC 51, the company created to run the club, went into voluntary liquidation, following year-on-year financial losses. The building itself was demolished in 2002 to make way for the building of an apartment block.[3] Despite its untimely and unfortunate demise due to drugs and gang violence, its early days are remembered with a fondness for the popular culture that was prevalent in the 1980s and 1990s. Its lifespan was quite short but its legacy remains as a cultural icon of the Manchester popular music scene.

New Order came out of the 1970s and 1980s post punk era, since some of the members had been in the punk-influenced group Joy Division. New Order was formed in 1980 and combined punk tradition with the new-wave electric synth sounds that were emerging at the same time. The band became the key signing for Factory Records and was the main finance behind the Hacienda. The group split in 1993 but reconvened in 1998 and have split up and made come-backs in 2001 and 2007, continuing to offer the occasional appearance. The Happy Mondays was another influential band. Originating from nearby Salford, their front man was Shaun Ryder and they offered their own distinctive style of rock music. They were discovered by Hacienda and Factory Records boss Tony Wilson and were signed by the FAC51 label in 1985. They disbanded in 1993 but have made come-backs in the 2000s. Despite the Hacienda's demise, its legacy inspired up and coming bands that came to fame in the 1990s, including the Gallagher brothers in the form of Oasis, have won a number of musical accolades since then, but in 2009 their story came to a close when the band split. Another band that came to fame at the turn of the 1990s was Take That, whose members included Gary Barlow and Robbie Williams. Their rise to fame was dramatic, and pressures within the band led to the departure of Robbie Williams, who subsequently went solo, and shortly afterwards, in 1996, the band split. However, after a break of ten years, they came back together, though Robbie William's role in the reconciliation was short lived. In recent times, a more mature Take That comprising three of the original members continues to enjoy musical success.

From the 1980s to the present day, Manchester has continued to improve its cultural identity by turning many of its former redundant buildings into modern centres of art and culture. For instance, the Great Northern was a former railway goods warehouse that has been transformed with retail outlets, high-quality restaurants and car parking. Here, the building has retained its Victorian façade that is representative of its heritage and has been carefully restored so as to reflect both old and new. It is testimony to more recent policy of preserving the heritage of the city rather than continuing the one adopted in the 1970s of removing anything that was a reminder of Manchester's industrial past. Behind the Great Northern, at the end of Deansgate, is Beetham Tower, one of the tallest buildings in the country. Completed in 2006, the forty-seven-floor building it is a mixture of apartments and the Hilton Hotel, which takes up half of the building. It is also believed to have the highest home in the UK, and is a symbol of the cosmopolitan and global status of Manchester. Another

72 A night at the Hacienda. (Courtesy of Alamy)

73 The Great Northern building, with Beetham Tower in the background.

fine example of regeneration is that of the Printworks on Withy Grove, which was a former 1870s newspaper printing house that produced papers such as the *Manchester Evening Chronicle*, and northern editions of nationals such as the *Daily Mirror* and *Daily Telegraph* for over a hundred years, and is another building which has been saved and turned into a modern-day leisure complex of restaurants, bars and cinemas. It has had a number of names during its time as a printing press, from Withy Gove Printing House, Chronicle Buildings, Allied House, then Kemsley House, the latter two names reflecting the changes in businesses that ran it, then in 1924 it became Allied Newspapers then Kemsley Newspapers in 1943. It ceased printing in 1985 and was purchased by the media tycoon Robert Maxwell and renamed Maxwell House, but during the early 1990s, and following Maxwell's death and the collapse of his empire, the building remained derelict until after the IRA bombing of 1996 when, as part of the overall reconstruction of the affected area, the building was incorporated into the city centre master plan. It opened in November 2000 with singer Lionel Richie and former Manchester United manager Alex Ferguson guests at the opening event. Again, the building has been sympathetically restored both inside and out and the interior still reminds the visitor of its printing press past.

Overlooking the Printworks is one of Manchester's more unusual buildings. Currently the National Football Museum, it was originally called Urbis (and is still referred to as such by locals) to reflect its role as a museum of urban life.

74 The Printworks.

75 The Urbis building, from the end of the building, currently the National Football Museum.

It began in 2002 as part of the redevelopment of Exchange Square following on from the 1996 devastation. Its first role as a museum of urban life did not succeed as planned, since visitor numbers were disappointingly low, and the building faced financial uncertainty. Admission charges were scrapped, and this did increase visitors for a time, but not enough on a long-term basis, and it was acknowledged that the initiative simply had not worked. It eventually closed in 2010 and an opportunity arose to house the National Football Museum, which in 2012 relocated from its original home at the Deepdale stadium in Preston. Its architecture is incredibly striking and modern, and despite it being located in the medieval quarter the mix between old and new somehow works.

Theatreland

Manchester is home to a number of prominent theatres that offer a range of performances for all kinds of different tastes, both modern and more traditional. Two of the more original theatres include the Palace Theatre and the Manchester Opera House. The Palace Theatre, located at the top of Oxford Street and the corner of Whitworth Street, opened in May 1891. It was designed by Alfred Darbyshire and cost around £40,000. The opening performance was a ballet of Cleopatra, but in the early days the theatre did not make much impact and was lucky to survive, as it appeared that the type of

77 Manchester's Palace Theatre. (Courtesy of Google Maps)

performances it offered were not all that popular and created financial difficulties. The theatre decided to broaden its repertoire and appeal, turning more
to music hall style of entertainment which improved both ticket sales and the
theatre's profits. Here, artists such as Little Tich, Lillie Langtry, Danny Kaye,
Gracie Fields, Charles Laughton, Judy Garland, Noël Coward and Laurel and
Hardy took to the stage in a full and vibrant theatre. It could originally house
around 3,600 people but after renovations in 1913 this was reduced to around
2,600. During the 1920s and 1930s, it became noted for musical productions
and pantomime.[4] In September 1940, the Palace Theatre took a direct hit from
a German bomb during the raids of that year. It recovered from this but, by
1970, audience numbers declined and it once again found itself struggling to
survive, as did in many live venues of the time, and it again faced closure. The
Arts Council came to its rescue and after major refurbishments the Palace
Theatre came back to life as an arts venue. It continues to this day, offering
a host of shows, including some that tour from the West End in London, and

it attracts well-known celebrities in its performances. The Manchester Opera House opened in 1912 and was originally called the New Theatre, changing to the New Queen's Theatre in 1915 then turning to the Opera House in 1920. After many years, it closed in 1979 when, as with the Palace Theatre, cultural venues suffered in the economic decline of the 1970s. It then became a bingo hall, hardly fitting a building of its stature and cultural significance. However, befitting the building's status, it returned to its roots as a theatre and is still open today, offering a range of entertainment but particularly focusing on musicals, and has hosted *West Side Story* and *The Phantom of the Opera*.

There are two theatres in Manchester that are slightly more unusual in their origins and remit. The first of these is the Royal Exchange Theatre. It was once 'the largest room in the world', as the trading centre for the cotton industry, but a new use had to be found for the building. The great hall was the epicentre of cotton trading and this continued until 1968 despite the demise of the cotton trade after the First World War and being struck by bombing during the Second World War. In fact, the last day's trading figures can still be seen on the large display board. The Cotton Exchange, once the visible representation of Manchester's role in world trade, was closed, and the building faced a bleak future until a theatre company decided to occupy it in 1973 and try it out for performances. This was a promising start to a totally new concept in theatrical entertainment, and the Royal Exchange Theatre Company was officially formed in 1976. Ever since, the theatre has put on many performances of Shakespeare and other classical works and it attracts some of our finest actors. It is a unique theatre experience in which the theatre and seating are in a capsule in the centre of the great hall and performances are experienced 'in the round', giving the audience a sense of being part of the performance. It was unfortunate in facing damage for the second time due to bombing with the 1996 attack. After two years of renovation the building opened once more. The Exchange building is also home to a fine array of shops both in an arcade and around the perimeter of the building, looking onto St Ann's historic square.

Manchester Central Reference Library, which opened in 1934, contained a 300-seat lecture theatre located in the basement of the building. In 1946, its use was extended by the Manchester Corporation Act of 1946 which allowed it to be utilised more fully, and it became a proper theatre and proved successful in staging plays. The theatre closed in 2010 for refurbishments. In addition, the Cornerhouse is an arts venue located at the corner of Oxford Road Station which has been well-known over the years for independent films. It mainly sup-

78 Manchester Opera House.

ported up-and-coming artists and held many art exhibitions for new talent. For example, it was noted for hosting the premier of Quentin Tarantino's film *Reservoir Dogs*, and was the first to exhibit the work of the artist Damien Hirst. In April 2012, the Cornerhouse and the Library Theatre Company merged to create the Greater Manchester Arts Centre Ltd (GMAC). This merger was the beginning in the creation of HOME, an international centre for contemporary visual art, film and theatre.

The Apollo Theatre in Ardwick was built in 1938 as an art deco-styled cinema and variety entertainment venue, though by the 1970s it had closed its cinema and became a concert venue hosting a number of popular music events. The 3,500 capacity offers a smaller pop concert venue, unlike the Manchester Arena, which is a modern, purpose-built venue opened in 1995, and holds around 20,000 people. The Arena was originally sponsored by Nynex and later the *Manchester Evening News*. It was built in preparation for the 2000 bid for the Olympics and funded by the government and the European Regional Development Fund. However, despite this Olympics bid being unsuccessful, the investment was not in vain since the arena became part of the successful 2002 Commonwealth Games bid where it hosted a number of sporting events. It continues to hold major sporting activities such as boxing matches, basket-ball, and ice hockey. It is home to three major sports teams, the Manchester Storm and Manchester Phoenix Ice Hockey teams and Manchester Giants basketball team. Boxing matches have included appearances by the likes of Amir Khan, Mike Tyson and David Haye. It was also in 2002 that it was classed as 'International Venue of the Year', and Europe's Favourite Arena of the Year in 2008. Since its opening, it has attracted many of the world's artists, such as Pavarotti, Kylie Minogue, Lionel Richie, Cher, and local band Simply Red. Local comedian Peter Kay is also a regular at the Arena, and on one occasion in 2010 he appeared on twenty consecutive nights, which is a record for the venue. It continues to be one of the busiest concert venues in the world and attracts the world's greatest stars, as well as a host of other events.

Sporting Success

During the 1990s, Manchester placed bids for number of major global games, twice unsuccessfully for the Olympics and a successful bid to host the Commonwealth Games. The first bid for the 1996 Olympics was largely driven by private companies which saw the investment potential of bringing such an event to the region. The City Council eventually became involved but it has to be said that support both locally and in general was poor. Manchester? Olympics? Both words just did not go in the same sentence for most people, particularly when the likes of Sydney were flaunting their sunny harbour and famous Opera House. Consequently, the bid failed, due to disinterest amongst central government and competing with cities that, on paper, had much more to offer. However, in true Mancunian style, the ambition to host something global did not deter some, including Sir Bob Scott who was instrumental in all the bids. Scott had been influential in the city for some time and had done much to promote cultural venues, when he was connected to the Royal Exchange Theatre, the Palace Theatre and the Opera House. He was also founder of the Cornerhouse and has been on the Board of the former Central Manchester Development Corporation.[5] A subsequent bid for the 2000 Olympic games was submitted, and whilst again it did not succeed, it was much better in its remit and the support was more widely offered by local and central government. A site on the edge of the city centre, known as Eastlands, had been chosen for major regeneration. The Eastlands site, just a short distance from Ancoats, had once been packed with industry, such as Manchester Steel and other engineering plants, but these had all closed and many thousands had become unemployed. Districts in the immediate vicinity such as Bradford, Beswick and Clayton were also very much deprived. In 1992, the East Manchester Regeneration Strategy provided the basis for a new

79 The former 2002 Commonwealth Stadium, currently the Etihad and home of Manchester City FC.

80 The new Co-operative Building, opened in 2013 as part of the NOMA project that has redeveloped the northern part of Manchester city centre.

community of sporting facilities, housing and retail outlets and hosting a major sporting event was likely to make a potential huge return on this investment. Plans included a new main sports stadium, cycling velodrome and athletes' village. It was shortly after this failed bid that Manchester was invited to bid for the 2002 Commonwealth Games which this time was successful and a huge accolade for the city. The legacy of this has meant major investment in the area, with the main stadium renamed the Etihad, the home of Manchester City, who moved from their former Maine Road ground, and which has also recently developed an impressive football training academy. The cycling velodrome, which was opened in 1994, is now the home of national cycling and has provided facilities for a number of athletes who have gone on to win many medals at subsequent Olympics and other global sporting events. At the same time, there were plans for new swimming facilities, and the Aquatics Centre, located on Oxford Road in the university corridor, was opened in 2000 in preparation for the 2002 Commonwealth Games. It is jointly owned by the City Council and both of Manchester's universities and is now a major facility both for the community and training aspiring professional athletes.

Previous chapters have shown the development of football in the region, and in modern times Manchester has been home of two of the biggest football clubs in the world. We have seen the story of the city's footballing heritage, with the game developing in the region from the end of the nineteenth century and becoming one of the key leisure pursuits for Mancunians. Manchester United's home has predominantly been Old Trafford for most of the club's life, and Sir Alex Ferguson managed the club between 1986 and 2013, making him one of the most successful managers of his generation. The club's domination continued through the 1980s and 1990s, largely under the direction of Ferguson, and he in fact broke Busby's record at the club. It is ironic that in a game that has such massive managerial turnovers, MUFC have had just two of the most successful managers in football in half a century of the club's existence.[6] Manchester City has had a more chequered history in its rise to the top but are nonetheless one of the best sides in the country. Manchester City stayed at Maine Road until 2003 when, shortly after the Commonwealth Games, it moved to the Eastlands stadium.[7] In 1996, Old Trafford held a number of football matches as part of England's hosting of the 1996 European Cup championships, which ended in the city with a concert by local bands M People and Simply Red. Even the bombing of Manchester in the middle of the tournament did not affect the spirit in the city, and it was very much business as usual.

Conclusion

From the 1980s, Manchester has seen significant regeneration and has regained the status it once had during the nineteenth century as a global player in the economy and as a cosmopolitan and vibrant city. Some of the regeneration was vital after the depressing 1970s, and this did indeed make progress, but a large part came as a result of the sudden and devastating bombing of 1996. The city has responded to both negative events with a spirit and determination and the city is now a place that recognises its industrial heritage but at the same time is moving forward as one of Britain's most important cities. From 2015, Manchester began a journey towards a new phase of independence in its governance and stature through its status as a 'Northern Powerhouse', in which the great cities of Northern England establish themselves as key self-governed regions that manage their own affairs away from Whitehall and the London-centric culture that has been seen to have hindered their progress in the past.

Notes

1   Bamford, *Manchester*.
2   Bamford, *Manchester*.
3   Haslam, D., *Manchester: the story of the pop cult city* (Fourth Estate, 1999).
4   http://palacetheatremanchester.net/
5   http://news.bbc.co.uk/1/hi/england/3039894.stm [accessed 28 December 2016].
6   manutd.com
7   mancity.com

TOWARDS A NORTHERN POWERHOUSE

W e have been on a journey to reflect upon the story of one of the UK's most notable cities, and it has been one of early beginnings, developing trade and commerce and an infrastructure to support this that was ahead of its time, constantly having to keep pace with its own successful progress. The story is as much about the people of Manchester as the place, and they have been shown to be industrious, hard-working, creative, and resilient.

The story began with Roman Mancunium which was of strategic importance to the conquerors, in part because of its geography, on an outcrop close to two rivers, the Irwell and the Medlock, which provided resources and a tactical place for the development of a military garrison. There are few obvious remains of the Roman occupation, though what has been preserved can be found in Castlefield's Roman Gardens and a few artefacts in local museums. The Roman legacy that is often not appreciated is the initial development of the road infrastructure that we use today. After the Romans left, the story of the area became unclear, as the Castlefield site fell into ruins, and much of this intervening time is obscure, yet the town re-emerges further upstream from the River Irwell, as the Manor of Manchester and the church that was to eventually become the cathedral formed during medieval times. Here, the medieval village developed into an early modern town and today is the heart of Manchester's shopping, ecclesiastic and cultural district, housing Chetham's school and library as well as more modern features. It is here that Manchester grew into the city we know today. In medieval Manchester the Lord of the Manor governed according to the old feudal system common to England at that time, yet there were glimpses of more modern forms of government developing, and the Lord of the Manor and his servants had a more equitable relationship than that seen in other parts of the country, through the Greater Charter of 1301. It was during this time that markets and fairs become a feature of trade and commercial activity and people regularly visited from the surrounding villages.

Early Modern Manchester developed its infrastructure even further with the arrival of hospitals, prisons, and education. Humphrey Chetham's school went from strength to strength, and William Hulme added to this with the Manchester Grammar School. The development of the textiles trade emerged at this time, for which Manchester would ultimately become famous. European wars provided an opportunity for the region which could not have been predicted, and what was initially an unsettling time for Flemish weavers proved to be a major opportunity for Manchester, as the weavers came to escape persecution and settle here, bringing a range of craft experience with them. The seeds of the textiles industry were sown as their skills were passed to the locals.

The Civil War during the 1640s affected all of the country and came to Manchester in the form of a week-long siege, which fortunately passed without major incident, and support for the Parliamentarians against the monarchy remained. Politics in the region became complicated and divisive, and from the late 1700s Manchester began to be noted for its radical politics, first through sympathies for the Stuart monarchy, and later in the century as industrialisation began to affect how people worked and lived. Political divisions were often aired in local inns, where hostelries were noted as being for one side or another in political debates.

Industrial progress truly took off during the middle of the eighteenth century and continued into the nineteenth century and beyond. At that time, merchants were forging commercial networks with surrounding towns with Manchester as the focal point. Increasingly, cotton replaced wool as the main form of textile production and a whole host of trades sprung up from cotton spinning and weaving, including engineering, chemicals and dyeing processes. Manchester emerged as a cosmopolitan town, where local merchants were trading abroad and welcoming overseas visitors to the city. The infrastructure and institutions of the town developed rapidly, with factories, housing, commercial centres such as the Manchester Exchange, and a transport system that was vital for the success of trading activity. Roads and canals were engineered and railways started operation during the 1830s. However, industrial progress had its down side. The large number of people coming into Manchester from the surrounding towns and villages to find work led to poor housing, cramped conditions and health problems. Factory masters treated their workforces badly. Politically, working-class people were a group with no voice and influenced by events on the continent, and the French Revolution created the right conditions for dissent, and even the possibility of revolution here too. Manchester had always been a place at the forefront of politics and at the end of the eighteenth and into nineteenth century Manchester was rife with political discontent and the authorities trying to control an ever difficult situation.

Manchester was a society very much based on class – you were working class or middle class, or rarely upper class. Every aspect of your life was governed by your economic place in the pecking order. One observer who enlightens our view of this time was Friedrich Engels, whose 1840s work *The Condition of the Working Class in England* eloquently brought to life how the working class of Manchester lived and worked. Yes, Engels was writing from one particular perspective, and some have argued that much was distorted in translation from his original German manuscript, however, the fact that his writings are still studied in universities today is testament to the importance of his work in the historical record of Manchester. Was Manchester all bad, with only poverty and grime? Well, certainly not amongst the middle class, who enjoyed the opportunity to make money and engage in civic, cultural and political circles. They subscribed to a number of institutions of learning, arts and science. Some would argue they helped the working class, too, in attempting to raise educational standards, though others question middle-class motives in trying to bring working-class standards to their own level. However, the distinction was clear, and working-class people worked very hard for little reward, and this influenced various political movements and spilled over during the Peterloo Massacre of 1819, the most notable date in Manchester's history. Manchester by now had become the centre of radical political thinking, putting pressure on the government to review the franchise and working people's democratic rights. It took some time, from the seeming failure of the Great Reform Act of 1832, to the Second Reform Bill of 1867, right through to the suffrage campaigns of the early twentieth century. Only then was equality finally granted for working people and women, and what a price had been paid!

The second half of the nineteenth century was a much quieter affair, economically, socially and politically for Manchester. Post-1850, even working-class people were that bit better off and whilst full equality was not yet present in society, there had been progress that led to a calmed optimism. It was around this time that Manchester changed from a town to a city, and the Art Treasures Exhibition at Old Trafford showcased the region's trade, commerce and cultural life. The economy was less turbulent than in the first half of the century and even working people had a little more in their pockets, and a host of legislation that was passed during the 1840s had improved their lives. The Second Reform Act in 1867, whilst again not allowing the vote for everyone, was a further step toward full emancipation, and the suffragettes were about to commence their campaigns for greater equality of the sexes. Whilst discussions about the rights of women had been aired for some time, most notably through Mary Wollstencraft's *Vindication of the Rights of Woman*, there was little point pursuing their cause when the majority of men were still fighting for a political voice.

By the turn of the twentieth century, Manchester had become a modern city and a rapidly growing conurbation. The suffragette campaign had its heart in Manchester, where Emmeline Pankhurst, and daughters Sylvia and Christabel, displayed a more militant form of the women's movement, certainly until the First World War broke at any rate. The suffragettes campaigned bravely and yet there is debate even today whether it was women's roles in the First World War that was the major factor in them obtaining the franchise or whether it was already on its way regardless. The region recruited many to the Pals regiment to fight bravely on the front line. The city was affected again by war, this time in the Second World War, which saw a number of key places in and around the city destroyed, and during the air raids of 1940 the region was particularly badly hit. By 1913, the cotton industry was in terminal decline, but the region's engineering capability was instrumental in both world wars as Avro, for example, provided aircraft and technology which was vital to the country's war effort. Post-war Manchester, its people and cultural life were so beautifully captured by one of the region's most famous sons, L.S. Lowry. His portrayal of working-class life depicts the same industriousness that was witnessed in the Industrial Revolution. He captured working-class leisure and life in paintings such as *Going to the Match*, where football was the main male working-class form of leisure on a Saturday afternoon.

The governance of Manchester, primarily through the City Council, has been instrumental in shaping the modern city and, with the election of Andy Burnham as mayor, Greater Manchester will continue to strive for greater autonomy from London. The City Council that came into existence in 1974 following the reorganisation of local government continues to be controlled by the Labour Party, and for the last twenty years has been led by Sir Richard Leese, who became council leader in 1996. Leese has extensive local government experience, and prior to this was deputy leader from 1990 until he took up the leadership role, and he had previous experience in both education and finance. He has been accompanied by Sir Howard Bernstein for most of his leadership, who has acted as Chief Executive since 1998. Both have been instrumental in bringing investment to the city and have made wide contributions to the redevelopment of Manchester, particularly following the 1996 bombing. Leese, along with Baroness Beverley Hughes were recently appointed deputy mayors.

Manchester continues to strive for increased autonomy, as part of the Northern Powerhouse agenda the Conservative government began in 2015 by providing the large northern cities a chance of increased autonomy in the process of rebalancing power and wealth that has always been centred on London and the south-east. Going forward, Manchester is a key part of the Northern Powerhouse agenda, in which transport, health, science and innovation, and devolution in the form of an elected mayor for Greater Manchester are all key components. Mancunians will hopefully enjoy better road and rail services in one of the busiest commuter regions, which has lagged behind in investment. By introducing an elected mayor for Greater Manchester, new powers and autonomy allows Manchester to govern its own affairs and economy more effectively. In November 2014, an agreement was signed to give Greater Manchester more powers in transport, housing, policing, health and planning. On 1 April 2016, Greater Manchester took control of its health budget to the tune of £6 billion and for the first time local government has been enabled to tailor its finances directly to the needs of its local population. Everyone watches with anticipation to see how this policy works out and whether Manchester does indeed deliver a new concept in healthcare based on managing its own resources more effectively at the local level. Modern Manchester is such a mix of the old and new, and is one of the most cosmopolitan cities in the UK. It is both politically and culturally influential, but at the same time is a city striving to maintain its own identity when Great Britain is criticised for being too London-centric. The people of Manchester, both past and present, should rightly be proud of their achievements. For the first industrial city, the list of achievements is long: hosting two of the most famous football clubs in the world, having one of the biggest airports in the country, holding the Commonwealth Games and making two bids for the Olympics, and being one of the most concentrated areas of higher education in the country.

As this book closes, we pay tribute to the twenty-two people who died and over 100 injured as Manchester was once again struck by a bomb on 22 May 2017 at the Manchester Arena. The shock and pain felt in the city is palpable but its determination and spirit continues as the next story of Manchester is about to unfold.

BIBLIOGRAPHY

Books and Articles

Aikin, J., *A Description of the Country from Thirty to Forty Miles Around Manchester* (1795).

Ainsworth, R., *History of Ye Old Bull's Head Hotel, Old Market Place* (Arden Press, 1923).

Allen, R., *The Manchester Royal Exchange: two centuries of progress 1729–1921* (Published by the authority of the Board of Directors of the Manchester Royal Exchange, 1921).

Aston, J., *The Manchester Guide: A Brief Historical Description of the Towns of Manchester & Salford, the Public Buildings, and the Charitable and Literary Institutions* (Joseph Aston, 1804).

Aston, J., *A Picture of Manchester* (WP Aston, 1816).

Axon, W., *The Annals of Manchester* (John Heywood, 1885).

Bagwell, P.S., *The Transport Revolution from 1770* (Batsford, 1974).

Bailey, P., *Music Hall: the business of pleasure* (Open University Press, 1991).

Baines, E., *History of the County Palatine of Lancaster* (George Routledge & Sons, 1868).

Baines, E., *History of the Cotton Manufacture in Great Britain* (H. Fisher, R. Fisher & P. Jackson, 1835).

Baines, T., *Lancashire and Cheshire: past and present*, vol. 1 (Heritage Publications (1868 (2012)).

Baker, T., *Memorials of a Dissenting Chapel* (Simpkin, Marshall & Co., 1884).

Bamford, P., *Manchester: 50 years of change* (HMSO, 1995).

Barker, T.C., Gerhold, D., *The Rise and Rise of Road Transport, 1700–1990* (Cambridge University Press, 1993).

Barker, T.C. and Savage, C.I., *An Economic History of Transport in Britain* (Routledge, 1974).

Belchem, J., 'Manchester, Peterloo and the Radical Challenge', *Manchester Region History Review*, vol. 3(1) (1989) pp. 9–14.

Bent, J., *Criminal Life: Reminiscences of Forty-Two Years as a Police Officer* (John Heywood, 1891).

Best, G., *Mid-Victorian Britain 1851–1875* (Fontana Press, 1985).

Bowd, S., 'In the Labyrinth: John Dee and Reformation Manchester', *Manchester Region History Review*, vol. 19 (2008) pp. 17–43.

Bruton, F.A., *The Roman Fort at Manchester* (Manchester University Press, 1909).

Bryant, S., Morris, M., Walker, J.S.F., *Roman Manchester: a frontier settlement* (Greater Manchester Archaeological Unit, 1986).

Bush, M., *The Casualties of Peterloo* (Carnegie, 2005).

Camden, W., *Britannia*, (translated from latin by Edmund Gibson), (University of Adelaide e-books, 1722).

Caminada, J., *25 Years of Detective Life in Victorian Manchester,* Vols 1& 2 (1895).

Chartres, J. & Turnbull, G., 'Road Transport', in Aldcroft, D. and M. Freeman (eds.), *Transport in Victorian Britain* (Manchester University Press, 1983).

Chase, M., *Chartism: a new history* (Manchester University Press, 2007).

Cooke Taylor, *Notes of a Tour in the Manufacturing Districts of Lancashire* (Duncan & Malcolm, 1842).

Cooper, A.V., *The Manchester Commercial Textile Warehouse, 1780–1914: a study of its typology and practical development,* (PhD, Manchester Polytechnic, 1991).

Cordery, S., *British Friendly Societies, 1750–1914* (Palgrave, 2003).

Davies, A., Fielding, S., *Workers' Worlds: cultures and communities in Manchester & Salford, 1880–1939* (Manchester University Press, 1992).

Dyos, H. & Aldcroft, D., *British Transport: an economic survey from the seventeenth century to the twentieth* (Penguin Books, 1969).

Engels, F., *The Condition of the Working Class in England*, translated by W.O. Henderson & W.H. Chaloner (Blackwell, 1845 (1958)).

Evans, E., *The Great Reform Act of 1832* (Routledge, 1994).

Everett, J., *Panorama of Manchester and Railway Companion* (J. Everett, 1834).

Faucher, L., *Manchester in 1844: its present condition and future prospects* (Cass, 1844).

Frangopulo, N., *Rich Inheritance: a guide to the history of Manchester* (Manchester Education Committee, 1962).

George, A.D., 'A Note on A V Roe and the Brownsfield Mill, Ancoats', *Manchester Region History Review*, vol. 7. (1993), pp. 93–6.

Gosden, P., *The Friendly Societies in England, 1815–1875* (Manchester University Press, 1961).

Gregory, R., *Roman Manchester: the University of Manchester's Excavations within the Vicus, 2001–5* (Oxbow Books, 2007).

Gunn, S., *The Public Culture of the Victorian Middle Class: ritual and authority in the English industrial city, 1840–1914* (Manchester University Press, 2007).

Harland, J., *Collectanea Relating to Manchester and its Neighbourhood,* vol. 1 (Chetham Society, 1866).

Harland, J. *Mamecestre,* vol. LIII (Chetham's Society Publications, 1861).

Harland, J., *A Volume of Court Leet Records of the Manor of Manchester in the Sixteenth Century,* (Chetham's Society, 1864).

Hayes, L., *Reminiscences of Manchester from the year 1840* (Sherratt & Hughes, 1905).

Hanham, *Elections and Party Management* (Longmans, 1959).

Haslam, D., *Manchester: the story of the pop cult city* (Fourth Estate, 1999).

Hibbert Ware, S., *History of the Foundation in Manchester of Christ's College, Chetham's Hospital and the Free Grammar School*, vol. 1 (Thomas Agnew & Joseph Zanetti, 1830).

Hill, J., 'Manchester and Salford Politics and the Early Development of the Independent Labour Party', *International Journal of Social History*, vol. 26 (2), (1981), pp. 171–201.

Hindle, G.B., *Provision for the Relief of the Poor in Manchester, 1754-1826* (Chetham's Society, 1975).

Hollingworth, R., *Mancuniensis, or a History of the Towne of Manchester* (1839 (1656)).

Hueffer, F., *Ford Madox Brown: a record of his life and work* (Longmans, 1896).

Hunt, T., *Building Jersualem: the rise and fall of the Victorian city* (Phoenix Press, 2005).

Jennison, G., *Zoological Gardens, Belle Vue, Manchester* (1929).

Jones, B., Grealey, S., *Roman Manchester* (Sherratt for the Manchester Excavation Committee, 1974).

Kay, Shuttleworth, J., *The Moral and Physical Condition of the Working Classes Employed in the Cotton Manufacture in Manchester* (James Ridgeway, 1832).

Kellett, J., *The Impact of Railways on Victorian Cities* (Routledge, 1969).

Kidd, A., *Manchester* (Edinburgh University Press, 2002).

Kift, D., *The Victorian Music Hall: culture, class and conflict* (Cambridge University Press, 1996).

Kondo, K., 'Lost in translation? Documents relating to the disturbances at Manchester, 1715', *Manchester Region History Review*, vol. 19 (2008) pp. 81–94.

Leber, M., 'The Remarkable Legacy of L.S. Lowry', *Manchester Region History Review*, vol. 1(2) (1987), pp. 13–22.

Linnaeus, Banks, G., *The Manchester Man* (E.J. Morten publishers), 1896).

Love, B., *Manchester as it is* (Love and Barton, 1839).

Manchester Corporation Transport Department, *A Hundred Years of Road Passenger Transport in Manchester* (1935).

Mortimer, J., *Mercantile Manchester: past and present*, (Palmer Howe, 1896).

Pankhurst, E., *My Own Story* (Hesperus Classics, 2015).

Parkinson-Bailey, J., *Manchester: An Architectural History* (Manchester University Press, 2000).

Pergam, E., *The Manchester Art Treasures Exhibition of 1857: entrepreneurs, connoisseurs and the public* (Ashgate, 2011).

Pickering, P., *Chartism and the Chartists in Manchester* (Palgrave, 1995).

Poole, R., *Wakes Holidays and Pleasure Fairs in the Lancashire Cotton District, c.1790–1890* (PhD thesis, Lancaster University, 1985).

Poole, R., *Popular Leisure and the Music Hall in Nineteenth Century Bolton* (Centre for North-West Regional Studies, 1982).

Prentice, A., *Historical Sketches & Personal Recollections of Manchester 1792–1832* (Cass, 1970).

Redford, A., *Manchester Merchants and Foreign Trade,* vol. 1 (Manchester University Press, 1934).

Roeder, C., *Roman Manchester* (Richard Gill, 1900).

Rose, J., *The Intellectual Life of the British Working Classes* (Yale University Press, 2001).

Russell, *Popular Music in England 1840–1914: a social history* (Manchester University Press, 1997).

Scott, R., *The Biggest Room in the World: a short history of the Manchester Royal Exchange* (Royal Exchange Theatre Trust, 1976).

Slugg, J., *Reminiscences of Manchester Fifty Years Ago* (Cornish, 1881).

Simon, S., *A Century of City Government: Manchester 1838–1938* (George Allen & Unwin, 1938).

Stancliffe, F.S., *John Shaw's* (Sherratt & Hughes, 1938).

Stedman, M., Manchester PALS (Leo Cooper, 2004).

Stevenson, J., *British Society 1914 to 1945* (Pelican, 1984).

Stobart, J, 'Manchester and its region: networks and boundaries in the eighteenth century', *Manchester Region History Review*, vol. 19 (2008), pp.66–80.

Swindells, T., *Manchester Streets and Manchester Men* (5 vols) (J.E. Cornish, 1906–08).

Tait, J., *Medieval Manchester and the Beginnings of Lancashire* (Sherratt & Hughes, 1904).

de Tocqueville, A., *Journeys to England & Ireland* (Faber and Faber, 1958).

The Ancient Ballad of Tarquin reprinted in 1808 by J. Aston.

Toulmin-Smith, L., *The Itinerary of John Leland in or about the years 1535–1543* (George Bell & Sons, 1909).

Turner, M., 'Local Politics and the Nature of Chartism: the case of Manchester', *Northern History*, vol. 45(2) 92008), pp. 323–45.

Vernon, J., *Politics and the People: A Study in English Political Culture, 1815–1867* (Cambridge University Press, 1993).

Wadsworth, A., Mann, J., *The Cotton Trade and Industrial Lancashire, 1600–1780* (Manchester University Press, 1965).

Walton, J., *Lancashire: a social history* (Manchester University Press, 1987).

Whitaker. J., *The History of Manchester*, vol. 1 (Dodsley, White & Lowndes, 1771).

Wildman, C., *The 'Spectacle' of Interwar Manchester and Liverpool: urban fantasies, consumer cultures and gendered Identities* (PhD thesis, University of Manchester, 2007).

Willan, T., *Elizabethan Manchester* (Manchester University Press, 1980).

Woodman, D., *The Public House in Manchester and Salford, c.1815–1880* (PhD thesis, Leeds Metropolitan University, 2011).

Wyborn, T., 'Parks for the People: the development of public parks in Victorian Manchester', *Manchester Region History Review*, vol. 9 (1995), pp.3–14.

Websites

baesystems.com
barbirollisociety.co.uk
bbc.co.uk
british-history.ac.uk
Coop.co.uk
gaskellsociety.co.uk
houseoffraserarchive.co.uk
iwm.org.uk
manchestereveningnews.co.uk
manchester.ac.uk
manchesterairport.co.uk
mancity.com
manutd.com
oxforddnb.com
palacetheatremanchester.net
rncm.ac.uk
victorianweb.org
workhouses.org.uk

Newspapers

Manchester & Salford Advertiser
Manchester Courier
Manchester Observer
Manchester Times
Northern Star
Poor Man's Guardian

Directories and Reports

(1831) The Complete Account of the Population of Great Britain (348), and (1901) Census of England and Wales [Cd.616], *House of Commons Parliamentary Papers.*

Court Leet Records for the Manor of Manchester, vol. VI (Henry Blacklock & Co. 1888).

The Statues, (Volume II), from the Eleventh Year of King George the Third to the First and second Years of King George the Fourth (London, 3rd ed. 1950), pp. 702–3.

Baines, E., *History, Directory and Gazetteer of the Palatine County of Lancashire* (W. Wales, 1825).

Pigot & Dean Trade Directory of Manchester & Salford for 1821/2 (Pigot & Dean, 1822).

Slater's Trade Directory for Manchester and Salford (1841).

Whellan's Directory for Manchester and Salford (1852).

INDEX